Oh, My Captiva
By Svea Scott

A history of Captiva Island

ISBN: 978-0-578-79162-3

Published by Book Baby

www.bookbaby.com

Copyright @ 2020 by Svea Scott

Revised 3/21

ACKNOWLEDGMENT:

I first would like to thank my great grandfather and great grandmother for finding this wonderful place that so many people enjoy.

I also would like to thank my late mother Julia Elizabeth Dickey Scott for whom this book is dedicated.

There are so many people to thank.

Myra Roberts, my dear friend for letting me use her art to illustrate the book.

My Friend Stephanie Bissett for writing the forward.

Alanna Reed for being my editor.

My cousin Terri McLaughlin who had a treasure trove of family photos

I also would like to thank the Jensen's for keeping the spirit and history of Captiva alive for all to enjoy.

FOREWARD BY STEPHANIE BISSETT

The year is 2020. You make your way across the infamous "Blind Pass Bridge". Tourists and locals alike enjoy the spectacular view, with their fishing lines dangling off the bridge, looking to hook the next Big Catch!

Some aspects of island life have changed since the time John Roby Dickey purchased 19 Gulf to Bay lots that ran from the south of Tween Waters Inn to the S curve that leads to the Green Flash. Many, however, have not….

First, Captiva remains a Sanctuary Island where much of the natural habitat has been untouched by developers. City ordinance does not allow any structure taller than the tallest palm tree, nor does it allow any chain restaurants or commercial development. The island life remains simple with only one post office, general store, only one four way stop sign located in the village, no traffic lights and no high-rise buildings. There is only one Chapel on the island, the beloved Chapel By The Sea, offering non-denominational services during season from November through April. Captiva Island is a tropical oasis with a small-town "Mayberry" feel.

The seven mile stretch along the Emerald waters of the Gulf of Mexico remain to be untouched in many aspects, not so much in others...like the population, and like the traffic during the snow-bird season! Once a hidden gem, Captiva is now a popular destination with visitors all over the United States, and even the world. Simplicity, a walk along the beach, seeing a beautiful sunset, and hooking that big fish are among the many reasons people flock to gorgeous Captiva Island.

The population has increased immensely. Currently, there are 200+ doors along Captiva Drive. This stretch of the island is called the Gold Coast, often known as "Millionaire Row". As vehicles make their way up the Gulf Drive, tourists can be seen looking at the significant mansions that lie along the gulf coast. The ever-popular questions are, "Who's house is that"? "Someone famous"??? In addition to the population increase, there has also been an increase in the size of property and homes being built. Nowadays, you pretty much need to purchase an existing structure, and bulldoze the house, start from scratch. The village, which is the heart of Captiva is now completely built out, and the popular South Seas Resort at the very north tip of the island offers 330 Acres of the very finest amenities & activities.

Oh, My Captiva, written by Ms. Scott, the great granddaughter of the first pioneer family shares her family's stories, experience, and life on the island as one of the first settlers. Back in the day, the properties were all "Gulf to Bay" offering one acre or more on the Gulf side and another acre or so on the Bay. Over the years the pieces were broken up, sold off, given away, and what have you. Ironically, now in the year 2020 many islanders are looking to piece them back together, attempting to recreate what once was. Then, and now, islanders and visitors alike still relish the simple, quiet, laid back island that so many find alluring and Captivating. Oh, My Captiva!

TABLE OF CONTENTS

Island Inn by Myra Roberts

Road Map by Myra Roberts

Chapter 1: The Beginning

John Roby Dickey found the islands of Sanibel and Captiva due to his brother suggesting he come there to help his sinus problem.

In 1894, John R. Dickey married Julia Hoffman. They had four children. Three boys and a girl. Herman (1896-1959), Clara Ellen (1898-1898) 4 mos., Carl (1899-1942) my grandfather and Ernest (1901-1968).

In 1905, when the boys were small, the Dickeys visited Sanibel along with their cook and houseboy. First, they traveled by train from Bristol, Virginia to Fort Myers, Florida. Then, they took a boat from Fort Myers to Bailey's old dock on the bay. Finally, they took a horse and buggy to the Hurricane House on Gulf Drive on Sanibel.

My great-grandpa and great-grandma had different hobbies. Julia Dickey enjoyed collecting shells. John Dickey loved to fish. He had to travel from Gulf Drive to Tarpon Bay in a horse and buggy. Today (2020) that trip takes 11 minutes. Imagine how long it took in 1905 by horse and buggy.

One day he decided to boat over to Captiva. He walked all over the island to find a piece of ground high enough to build a house.

In 1906 he purchased a piece of property one-half mile long on a section of the island that was high. The property ran gulf to bay from the north boundary where the road turns towards the Green Flash to the south boundary of Tween Waters.

The property was purchased from Herbert Binder who homesteaded Buck Key and Captiva.

The Dickey's began building their home in 1906. The original blueprint of the house was drawn in the sand. Paper blueprints were written, and contractors were hired.

The first one could not read blueprints. The second man said he could build the house if my great grandpa could tell him how many rooms he wanted and what each room would be used for. That would not do. So, on the third attempt, great grandpa hired Langley (Tobe) Bryant who could read blueprints.

The house was completed in 1906. My great-grandparents along with Herman, Carl and Ernest traveled back to the island that winter. They had traveled by train, then boat to the bulkhead off the shore of Captiva. The big boat could not go any closer to shore or it would bottom out.

The Dickeys took a smaller boat to shore, leaving all their belongings on the boat. They arrived on the island at night near where the Blind Pass Bridge is now. They had to walk the three and a half miles in the dark to the new house with only lamps to light their way. They arrived at the house, no lights, no beds, no running water and no bathrooms. My great-grandmother fixed up something to eat so they didn't go to bed hungry. The children were put to bed.

The sun had just come up the next morning when there was a knock on the door. John Dickey opened the door and there stood the man that had brought them on the boat. He had a sad look on his face. My great-grandfather asked him what was wrong. The man replied, "You would be sad too if your boat had sunk".

Realization came to my great grandfather. The boat that sank was the one that had all their belongings on it. The whole family went back down to the beach to see the boat submerged. They could only see the top of the deck. They rowed back to the boat to see what could be salvaged. The Dickeys had brought six months' worth of food. There were case after case of canned goods. All the labels had washed off. My great-grandmother was very frugal. If she opened cans that were all peaches, that is what they had.

They had barrels of salt, flour, sugar and rice. The water had penetrated the wooden barrels. The powders had to be dumped out on cloth and left to dry in the hot sun.

My great-grandmother had packed all her best clothes and linens. She had wrapped them in red and pink tissue paper. Because of the saltwater, everything had turned pink.

The only item that had remained dry was a cast net, which had been put in a waterproof container. The one thing that could get wet was the only thing that stayed dry.

The family moved in and got settled. Light was provided by lamps. Cooking was done on a wood burning stove. The cases of unlabeled canned goods were stored in the pantry. My great-grandmother called them "Mystery Meals" (as there was no way to tell what you were going to eat). A cistern was built to catch water for drinking.

There were no inside bathrooms; you had to use the four holer that was out on the dock when nature called.

When the Dickeys moved to the island, Herman was 10, Carl was 7 and Ernest was 5. The children missed so much school that their parents decided to hire a tutor, Miss Reba Fitzpatrick. She accompanied them in later years to and from Virginia. The Dickey Boys built her a small cottage that also served as their schoolroom.

The boys attended school with her until high school when they attended the Stetson Academy, and then, Stetson University (Herman in 1916 and Carl in 1919).

All the upstairs bedrooms had open ceilings so you could see the rafters. My great-grandmother hung muslin from the ceiling to make it beautifully white.

She also collected huge conch shells which she used to line the path to the beach. Conchs were later used to line the parking area at the house.

The years flew by quickly as she continued to collect shells and he continued to fish.

John R. Dickey with friends. Dr. John R. Dickey is the man to the right. A Days Catch. Dickey Family Photo

The Dickey Living room 1906. Showing the extensive collection of seashells collected by Julia Hoffman Dickey. Dickey Family Photo.

The Dickey property was divided into 19, 100-foot-wide sections, Gulf to Bay. This piece of land became known as the "John R Dickey Subdivision".

John R Dickey out for a day of fishing

Layout created by Author.

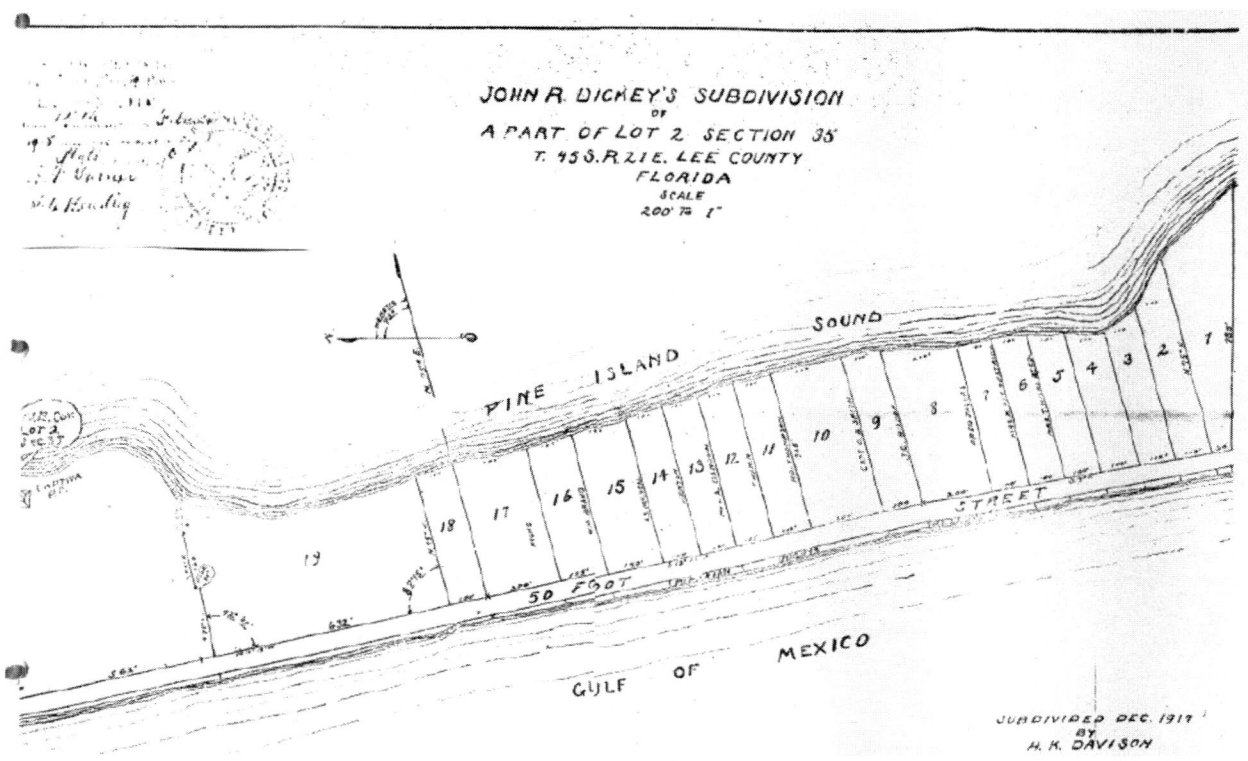

Map of the John R Dickey Subdivision.

As the years passed, my great grandfather gave away or sold off sections of land. Just to the south of the house, he sold to Doctor John Hicks and family.

Doctor Hick's home was an exact duplicate of the Dickey House. Dr. Hicks turned his house to face the north. The Dickey House faced the west.

Ding Darling by Myra Roberts

Chapter 2: NEW FACES OLD FRIENDS

1. Mr. & Mrs. Fayram

Teddy Roosevelt came to Captiva in 1914 and 1916. He, along with Colonel Russel Cole came on a barge. They came to the islands to find alternate sources of leather. They experimented with shark as well as manta ray. They started a company to find leather alternatives.

The barge they came on besides being a home away from home was also used as a laboratory for developing these new alternate sources of leather.

Roosevelt and Cole started the Ocean Leather Company on Sanibel Island. The leather that was created was used in WWI.

My second cousins Henry and Alma Connelly lived with the Dickeys after the death of their parents. When Roosevelt was staying on the barge, little Henry was swimming out in the gulf and swam up to the barge. He yelled out "Teddy!", and the former president came out and said, "come aboard young American".

So, Henry went on board the barge and spent the day with Roosevelt. Roosevelt also visited with my great grandparents.

Henry Connelly (1906-1996) and his sister Alma (1905-1996) had come to live with their grandparents when they were 7 and 6. The Dickey's daughter, Stella May (1882-1909) had been married to Joseph Henry Connelly (1878-1911).

2. James L. Loomis, Sr. (1920s)

In an interview for the book "True Tales of Old Captiva" James Loomis' son talked about the old days on the island. Mr. Loomis, Sr. came to the island in 1927 at the request of Harold Steiner and his wife to rest before he went back to Hartford, CT. Mr. Loomis was employed by Connecticut Mutual Insurance and he would come to a convention on the east coast each year. Mr. Steiner was the Secretary of Connecticut. He bought his home in the late 20s. There was not electricity on the island when the Loomis' bought the property. In fact, electricity did not come to the islands until the 1940s.

Mr. Loomis started building his house in 1937 and it was completed in 1939. The house was built by Mr. & Mrs. John Remington. They lived on the other side of the Blind Pass Bridge.

The Loomis' stayed at Tween Waters while their home was being built.

The beach at that time was 200 feet from the house. In 1900 when the Dickeys came to the island the beach was as wide as it would be in 1936.

Light was provided by Kerosene lamps. Water was provided by rainwater that was caught in cisterns. Or an artesian well could be dug. The water was sulfur and smelled like rotten eggs. Garbage was taken care of by digging holes in the ground. What a find it would be to dig up the front and back yards of the houses on the islands! I'm sure that they're a lot of Dickey Drug Co. bottles buried all over the island.

My mother Julia Dickey Scott saw her first movie at the Loomis' house. They had a huge upstairs room that was the children's playroom. It was a silent Charlie Chaplin movie.

Anne Morrow Lindbergh by Myra Roberts

3. Chapter 3: The Dickeys

John R. Dickey

John R. Dickey was born in 1856 in Independence, VA. His father was Stephen Miles Dickey (1825-1906), and his mother was Jane Drucilla Phipps (1833-1913). His father was a Civil War hero. He had an older brother named James Alexander. He received his education and pharmacology training in Bristol, Virginia. His brother was a physician. Dickey grew up on the family farm. He arrived in Bristol in 1875 at the age of 19. For a few years he worked with his brother at the City Drug Store.

In February of 1880, he went into partnership with Dr. Jere Bunting at Bunting Drug Store as a druggist located at #2 Ferguson Block in Bristol. Between February and May of 1880, they moved to #6 James Block on Main Street.

Their advertising consisted of promoting their "Southern Liver Regulator" patent medicine. By October of 1882, John R. Dickey and Jere Bunting had gone their separate ways. J.R. Dickey had formed his own company, J.R. Dickey & Company was a wholesale and retail druggist. His partner at the time was F.A. Hicks. Dr. Hicks provided the formula for the eye water that would later become his best-selling and longest lasting product.

Later advertisements in 1885 read "John R. Dickey manufacturing druggist." During this time, his prominent ads were for two products: Dickey's Indian Blood & Liver Pills and the Southern Liver Regulator. He had obtained all rights from Bunting for the last product.

In 1896, J.R. Dickey was in his Dickey Block Building, addressed at #10 Front Street where he remained for many years.

Dickey eventually constructed the famous Hotel "Tip Top". In 1898 there is mention of a drug store on Front Street, this possibly could be J.R. Dickey's business. At this time, his company was known as the J.R. Dickey Drug Co.

The Pure Food & Drug Act of June 30th, 1906 required he make some He made changes to his now leading medicinal product. He changed the "Old Reliable Eye Water" in order to follow the terms of the act.

Exactly when he began making the new eye wash is not known. Below is the transcript of the 1906 Food & Drug Act. Script is from the internet.

While Wiley was stumping for a law, muckraking journalists such as Samuel Hopkins Adams exposed in vivid detail the hazards of the marketplace. In fact, the nauseating condition of the meat-packing industry that Upton Sinclair captured in The Jungle was the final precipitating force behind both a meat inspection law and a comprehensive food and drug law. (A poster of the 1913 movie adaptation of Sinclair's novel is pictured at right, courtesy of the Sinclair Archives, Lilly Library, Indiana University, through James Harvey Young's Pure Food: Securing the Federal Food and Drugs Act of 1906.) Since 1879, nearly 100 bills had been introduced in Congress to regulate food and drugs; on 30 June 1906 President Roosevelt signed the Food and Drugs Act, known simply as the Wiley Act, a pillar of the Progressive era.

This act, which the Bureau of Chemistry was charged to administer, prohibited the interstate transport of unlawful food and drugs under penalty of seizure of the questionable products and/or prosecution of the responsible parties. The basis of the law rested on the regulation of product labeling rather than pre-market approval. Drugs, defined in accordance with the standards of strength, quality, and purity in the United States Pharmacopoeia and the National Formulary, could not be sold in any other condition unless the specific variations from the applicable standards were plainly stated on the label. Foods were not defined according to analogous standards, but the law prohibited the addition of any ingredients that would substitute for the food, conceal damage, pose a health hazard, or constitute a filthy or decomposed substance. Interpretations of the food provisions in the law led to many, sometimes protracted, court battles. If the manufacturer opted to list the weight or measure of a food, this had to be done accurately. Also, the food or drug label could not be false or misleading in any, and the presence and amount of eleven dangerous ingredients, including alcohol, heroin, and cocaine, had to be listed.

The bureau's regulatory emphasis under Wiley centered on foods, which he believed posed a greater public health problem than adulterated or misbranded drugs. Wiley generally held a dim view of chemical additives to foods, championing an approach that considered most to be unnecessary adulterants. On this he clashed often with Secretary of Agriculture James Wilson, and on occasion President Roosevelt himself had to decide government policy on food regulation. Wiley's personal administrative authority under the act was diluted early on when Wilson created a Board of Food and Drug Inspection in 1907 to establish agency policy in enforcing the law. Similarly, the creation of the Referee Board of Consulting Scientific Experts in the following year to advise the department on safety issues associated with food additives undercut Wiley's scientific authority. The bureau had been developing informal standards for many foods in collaboration with outside experts since 1903, an activity that continued after the 1906 act. However, courts differed on the role these informal standards could play in cases. Separate laws established standards for some specific foods, such as apples and butter, as well as for canned foods.

After Wiley's resignation in 1912, the bureau devoted more effort to drug regulation, with some emphasis on the so-called patent medicines. While the law was much clearer about drug standards than standards for foods, misbranding was the source of considerable controversy in the regulation of drugs. A year earlier the Supreme Court ruled that the law did not-- contrary to the government's interpretation--apply to false therapeutic claims. An amendment in the year of Wiley's resignation attempted to correct the language of the law. But it put the bureau in the difficult position of attempting to prove in court that manufacturers of drugs labeled with false therapeutic claims intended to defraud consumers. The bureau lost several cases against egregious products, but seizures of misbranded and adulterated drugs nevertheless increased in the 1920s and 1930s.

J.R. Dickey was prominently identified with Bristol's growth and progress. Although he was active and successful in business, much of his energy was given to educational, religious and philanthropic activities. He was on the board of Directors at Virginia Intermont College as well as being a deacon at his church.

He was one of the most prominent Baptist laymen in Virginia and for 29 years had been president of the board of trustees of Virginia Intermont College and contributed much to the success of the well-known Baptist Women's College.

He had been honored by his church in many ways. He was always interested in public affairs.

It is told by a family member who is now deceased about a Dickey relative who stole the eye water formula and fled to manufacture it somewhere else. There is a known embossed mold E.C. Dickey Red Eye water, Knoxville, Tennessee (E. being Everett). Whether this is the stolen formula is unknown.

A lesser-known Dr. Dickey's Eye water from Eufaula, Alabama is a product of J.R. Dickey's brother, James. It was sold by Cam Anderson who was one of James' salesmen. John's formula was not bottled until he opened his own business in 1885. James had been a doctor for about ten years.

Other products of J.R. Dickey were:

Dickey's Female Tonic & Regulator

Dixie Tasteless Chill Cure

Dickey's Old Reliable Eye Salve

Arabian Horse & Cattle Powder

Dickey Vegetable Confection

Dickey's Eureka Vermifuge

Dickey Blood Cure D.B.C.

Dickey Magic Nervine

Dickey Magic Relief

Dickey Cough Drops

Dickey German Cologne

Dickey Old Reliable Healing Ointment

Dickey Manhood Restorer

Dickey Indian Pile Ointment

Dickey White Oil

Dickey Japanese Toothache Drops

Dickey Magic Nerve & Bone Liniment

Dickey Syrup of Tolu, Tar & Wild Cherry (Tolu is a fragrant gum obtained from the bark of a leguminous South American tree, used in cough medicines, flavoring and perfumes. Tar is a dark, thick and sticky liquid with a sharp smell.)

Dickey Worm Confections

Dickey Bronchial Lozenges

Dickey Hair Vigor

Dickey Painless Corn Cure

Dickey Hair Renewer & Invigorator

Dickey Furniture Polish

Dickey Liver Regulator

Dickey Strengthening Porous Plaster

After J.R. Dickey's death in 1923, his sons Ernest and Herman continued operation of the eyewash business into the late 1950s. This took place on the second floor of the Front Street Dickey building where they also operated their investment company.

DR. J. A. DICKEY,

1. Dr. James A Dickey

Dr. James A Dickey was born in Grayson County, Virginia on September 13, 1849. He was a certified physician having attained his education at Emory and Henry College. He obtained his medical degree from Washington University in Baltimore. He established a practice in Grayson County in 1869. He was elected Treasurer in that county in 1873 and continued in that office until March 1875, when he resigned and moved to Bristol, Tennessee. By October 1875 he had purchased the drug stock of the recently deceased J.G. Pepper. He formed a partnership with a druggist named Wright. J.G. Pepper was the brother of Dr. C.T. Pepper for whom the drink Dr. Pepper is named.

Dr.J.A.DICKEY 1904

Dickey and Wright opened a drugstore on Main Street in Bristol. By 1879 their partnership had divided, and his business was named J.A. Dickey & Co. City Drug Co. at the sign of the Mortar & Eagle. (In 1880 included the names of two salesmen: J.C. (Cam) Anderson from Scott County, Virginia and T.M. Crandall in West Tennessee. During this time, John R. Dickey was associated with the company.)

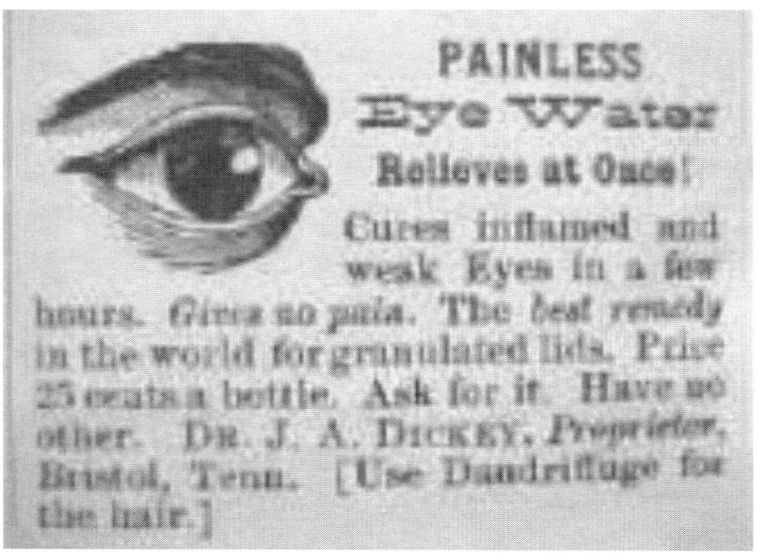

In 1888 he sold his interest in the company to Cam Anderson.

In 1882, James erected a house at 421 5th. Few of J.A. Dickey's bottles have remained. He was only in business for 12 years, whereas his brother stayed in business until his death in 1923. John's sons, Herman and Ernest kept the business open until the late 50s.

It was James who introduced his younger brother to the island of Captiva. John always had a bad sinus infection during the winter in Bristol, Virginia. James, being a physician as well as a druggist, suggested that John go south for the winter to help his sinus problem. John R. Dickey made his trip alone and found the fishing wonderful. And that brings me back to how it all started.

He returned in 1905 with his wife Julia Hoffman, who he had married in 1894. John and Julia had four children: Herman (1896-1959), Clara Ellen (1898-1898), my grandfather Carl (1899-1942) and Ernest (1901-1968).

In addition, they had four children from John Dickey's first marriage to Sarah James: Stella May (1882-1909), Virginia (1885-), John Roby Dickey, Jr. (1888-1935) and Florence (1899-1974).

The first trip as a family was in 1905. They brought the three boys with them.

They traveled by train from Bristol to Fort Myers. They spent the night in a hotel in Fort Myers. The next morning, they traveled by boat to the Bailey Dock. From there they took a horse and buggy to the Hurricane House on Gulf Drive.

My great-grandparents had very different interests. All he wanted to do was fish all day. She wanted to just spend her days on the islands' beaches. Traveling on horseback or buggy to Tarpon bay was getting old. While he was worrying about getting the best fish, great grandmother was collecting shells on the beach.

In 1904, great-grandfather purchased a piece of property from Herbert Binder, who homesteaded Captiva. The property was 2,640 feet long and went from the gulf to the bay. The property covered the area from the curve to the north to the south boundary of where Tween Water's is now. A beautiful two-story home was built on the south section of the property.

As I remember the house from my time spent there, there was a living room, dining room, linen room, kitchen and a bathroom on the first floor. On the second floor were four bedrooms and a bathroom. In later years the house was cut in two. A two-story section was moved down to the bay area and used as a caretaker's cottage. There was also a fifty-foot boathouse which was turned into a garage in later years.

My great-grandfather died in October of 1923. Great-grandmother continued to live in the house until her death in 1947.

Then, the house sat empty for five years. The drapes, hand crocheted rugs and her piano gathered dust.

My great-grandfather's will stated that the remaining 400 feet of property would be deeded to his three sons, Herman, Carl and Ernest. The main house was inherited by Ernest and his wife, Dorothy. The property to the south of the house was inherited by Herman and Carl. The property to the north of the house was inherited by Carl's children. This was my mother Julia Elizabeth Dickey (Scott), Mary Virginia Dickey (Barnes), Carl James Dickey, Jr., Clara Jane Dickey (Burlingham), and John Clark Dickey.

Dorothy Dickey (Douglas) was born in 1902 in Jefferson Ohio, the second child of William Edwin Douglas (1865-1936) and Elnora Crosby (1864-1927). She attended the Stetson Academy and graduated from Stetson University in Deland, Florida in 1924.

Ernest and Dorothy met at Stetson in the fall of 1919. They were married September 6, 1924 in Augusta, Georgia. Dorothy's father, Mr. Douglas had bought and refurbished an old home in Augusta for them especially for their wedding.

Ernest and Dorothy continued to visit Captiva whenever possible. Ernest and Herman managed the family business in Bristol. They still owned the Dickey Drug Company as well as a financial institution. They also owned a hotel called "The Teneva", which was located on the state line between Tennessee and Virginia.

Herman and his family lived in Bristol and only came down in the winter. Herman was married to Evelyn Turnquist (October 15, 1922-November 2, 1951) and they had one daughter, Marie. Evelyn died at the age of 54. They had been married 33 years.

Herman remarried to Bergot Dickey in Hendry County, Florida in 1953. They divorced in February 1958 in Lee County, Florida after five years of marriage.

Herman died on December 6, 1958 in Lee County, Florida. He was 63 years old. He was buried in Bristol, Virginia.

Marie Dickey continued to live on Captiva and in Bristol. Marie married Charles Arnold (Joe) Kalman October 3, 1942. She moved to New York City October 23, 1958. She and Joe had one daughter, Alexandra. Marie and Joe were divorced August 2, 1972 in Fort Myers, Florida. She continued to live on Captiva until her death on May 12, 2002.

Carl James Dickey, Sr. was born on July 22, 1897 in Bristol. His mother Julia was 32 and his father John was 40. His sister Clara Ellen was born in 1898 and only lived 4 months. Carl was one. His brother Ernest Hatcher was born April 8, 1901 in Bristol when Carl was three. His half-sister, Stella May, died in Tennessee when Carl was 12. Carl married Sara Elizabeth Clark.

Their daughter Mary Virginia was born May 3, 1925 in Lakeland, Florida. Their daughter Julia Elizabeth was born August 28, 1927 in Meadowview, Virginia. Carl James, Jr. was born June 18, 1930 in Fort Myers, Florida. Clara Jane was born March 14, 1935 in Fort Myers, Florida.

John Clark was born September 12, 1939. Clark was the only child that was born at home on Captiva Island. The rest had been born in the hospital.

Carl and his family continued to live on Captiva until 1942. Carl was a fishing guide and owned several boats that were rented out.

Carl James, Sr. died August 28, 1944 in Fort Myers, Florida. He died on my mother's 17th birthday. My mother (Julia Elizabeth's) 17th birthday. She and her older sister Mary The girls had walked downtown to the Arcade Theater to see a movie. Grandfather had been working downtown painting the McCroy's ceiling on a 14-foot ladder. He slipped and fell to the floor.

He was helped up by some of the clerks and the manager before he walked the several blocks back to their home at 2528 Third Street.

He told grandmother he was not feeling well and was going to go and lie down. She checked on him later and he told her that he was sorry that he had not had a chance to wish my mother a happy birthday. Carl, Jr. went in to check on him later and found him dead. Carl was only 14 at the time. He took the sheet and pulled it up over his head. The coroner came to the house and said that he must have had a massive brain bleed (stroke) from the fall. My mom got home from the movies and grandma had to tell her that her father was dead.

During the years from 1952-1954, Ernest paneled the first floor and modernized the kitchen. He added a bathroom and pantry off the kitchen. He put new screen on the bayside porch. On the second floor the great hall was paneled. Linen closets and cupboards were added. Space was taken from both ends of the trunk room to make closets for both east bedrooms. Storage space and a utility headboard were added in the master bedroom. All the floors in the house are the original plank floors. Some of the floors have been stained. Electrical wiring was added to the bayside porch and was run through a pipe. A few switches and outlets were added. Most of the lights are still turned on by using a pull chain.

As you approach the south porch there is an entrance into what was great-grandfather's office. This room became the first public library on the island. The library opened in 1918 and great grandmother was the first unpaid librarian. Mrs. Herman Dickey (Evelyn), Mrs. Hicks and Trula Hicks Rouse were the volunteers. Most of the Dickey books were donated to the Captiva Memorial Library.

The book boat began coming to the island in 1942. Once a week the boat docked at the old post office dock, making it convenient for the patrons of the post office to pick up books at the same time.

My great-grandfather had so many fishing friends that great-grandmother couldn't accommodate everyone. In 1910 he built the two-story Dickey Hotel. It had fourteen rooms with a lobby and a three-sided porch.

Dickey Hotel. Dickey Family Photo. This photo is also available at the Captiva Island Historical Society website.

Many fishing parties took place over the years. One of the visitors was then-president Teddy Roosevelt, but he did not stay at the hotel. Instead, he pitched a big tent on a barge in the bay. With him was Col. Russell Cole and a fishing guide named Jack McCan. They were studying different fish skins that could replace leather. The barge they were on provided not only a home, but a laboratory.

The Roosevelt party would come ashore to the only dock that was visible from the bay: The Dickey's Dock. "Teddy" and great-grandfather would sit on the porch and tell tall tales.

Great-grandfather had a great idea in the hotel. But he did not have the help to make it efficient. So, after three years of being open in 1940, Clarence E. Snyder asked if he could rent the building for his school.

In 1913, Mr. Snyder, who had a traveling school for boys, wanted to rent the hotel. He had moved his school from Asheville, North Carolina to Southwest Florida. He had originally planned to rent the Punta Rassa Hotel, but it burned down before he could move in.

He had to move his students to a small building on the southeast side of Buck Key. This building was not big enough for the school to expand, so Mr. Snyder approached great-grandfather to rent the hotel.

He ended up renting the hotel for the first year, then purchased the property. It was used as a school until 1924. I am not sure what the building was used for after that. The building burned down in 1936.

Dorothy and Ernest had four children, Ernest H. Dickey, Jr. (1925-1999), Margaret Dickey Geranmos (1927-1992), John Douglas Dickey (1936-1998), and Eleanor Dickey Orr Heacock

In 1954, Ernest and Dorothy spent their first extended vacation at the house.

In 1957, they replaced the bay dock. This was a little south of the original. The original dock was built in 1907. This dock was probably lost in the hurricane of 1926. All that was left was the track for the boat to be hauled into the fifty-foot boathouse. This boathouse was later turned into a garage and workshop.

I remember Aunt Dorothy pulling her Cadillac out of the garage and clipping the hibiscus hedge all the way up the drive. She would smile and say, "I do that all the time". My mother Julia Dickey Scott would tell me to sit on the other side of the car in case she clipped another vehicle.

To transgress a little, great-grandfather built a pier out in the gulf. It lasted two years, then was blown away by a hurricane.

So, he attempted it again. This one didn't last either. In 1912, boards from the pier washed up and were stacked against a banyan tree that was in the yard of Bud Beattie. By the fall of that year, the roots had surrounded the wood.

After 1956, Uncle Ernest and Aunt Dorothy came to the island each year. He suffered a fatal heart attack in 1968 in Bristol. Aunt Dorothy continued to live in the home up until her late 80s. She died at the age of 101 in Bristol.

In 1945 my cousin Marie Dickey Kalman wrote an article for Motor Boating Magazine. I am going to recount some of the stories that she told me that I know to be factual.

For starters, Sanibel and Captiva were just one big sandbar that turned into two. Blind Pass was first featured on a map in 1769. On a map from 1848 it is called Blind Pass. Over the years it has been open and closed too many times to remember. My mother (Julia Elizabeth Dickey Scott) called it: "The Lord giveth and the Lord taketh away." Sometime all the sand was on the Captiva side. Then, a storm would blow through and it would be on the Sanibel side.

In 1904 my great-grandparents returned to Sanibel. He had a bad sinus infection, and it was recommended that in the winter he travel south. Getting from Bristol to Fort Myers was not an easy task. You had to take the train from Bristol to Fort Myers. The train arrived too late to head to the islands that same day, so you had to spend the night in Fort Myers. I believe they stayed at the Hill House. In the morning they had to take a horse and buggy to the wharf where they would catch a steamer to Punta Rassa. Once at Punta Rassa, another boat would take them over San Carlos Bay to the dock that was next to Bailey's Store. They had to take a horse and buggy from there to the Matthews House.

Great-grandmother was in her element.

Sanibel had and has one of the best shelling beaches in the world. Every morning, great-grandmother would get up, have her breakfast, grab her straw hat and shelling basket and head for the beach. For her, Sanibel was a dream come true.

Great-grandfather on the other hand was not quite as happy as she. He had to drive a horse and buggy a mile over bumpy shell roads just to get to the boat. He would just get back to the hotel and remember something that he forgot on the boat and would have to turn around and go back. He would have to hitch up the horse again and head out. Both he and the horse were getting tired of this routine. Great-grandmother was getting concerned about him.

Well, Mrs. Matthews did not like her guests to be unhappy.

She took matters into her own hands and arranged a day trip for all her guests. A hotel picnic!

Captain Ormsby and his wife had a coconut plantation on Buck Key. This island was a little north of Sanibel. The picnic was to take place here.

The day arrived for the picnic. Two cartloads of guests bumped along the shell roads. They were surrounded on both sides by saber grass. It was so tall that you could not see over it. They would have to stop along the way for an alligator to cross the road. They had to travel eight miles. Imagine what the scenery was like in those days?

Great-grandmother had worn one of her new shorter dresses, which her husband almost had a fit over because he could see her ankles and so could everyone else. But here she was in her gloves, hat and parasol bumping along the eight-mile trip.

Around noon they finally got to the north point of Sanibel. Captain Ormsby crossed the narrow pass between Sanibel and Buck Key in his small motorboat. He could only carry four people at a time, so it took about four trips to get everybody across.

There was a beautiful two-story house as well as lush growth of coconuts, citrus trees, mulberry trees and Sapodilla. The plantation stretched from shore to shore on the small island.

Great-grandfather was more than a little interested in the layout of the small island. He had found a place where he could have his boat right at the front door. It was a perfect harbor. There was an island running parallel that kept the surf from pounding the shore. Everything seemed perfect. But when he told great-grandmother, she would not have it. There was NO BEACH to collect shells. She raised such a fuss that Captain Ormsby stepped in.

He pointed to the island across the water and said it would be perfect. It had a huge beach for shells. He said it was the most beautiful beach he had ever seen. It was as narrow as Buck Key in spots. He could keep his boat in the bay. She could continue shelling. They would have the best of both worlds.

Well, great-grandfather choked down the rest of his food. He borrowed Captain Ormsby's boat and rowed over to the island, spending the rest of the day walking its entirety. He stood on the highest point he could find. He could see the entire length of the island and that beautiful beach. When he turned around and looked in the opposite direction, he could see the beautiful bay. He had decided he wanted it. Now it was time to convince great-grandmother.

He started to tell her about that wonderful beach. She could picture herself out on that beach that only God had touched. She could see herself getting a shell collection that all her friends in Virginia would be impressed with. Great-grandfather did not have to do much talking.

They went back to the Matthews' and spent another week before he took her over to the island. The two of them tramped all over. They found the owner of the island. He had acquired it by living on the island to stake his claim of 160 acres straight from President Grover Cleveland. William Herbert Binder or Tom as he was called. (See Chapter 8 for more on Herbert Binder.)

No one knew where he came from. He was kind of strange. He was very smart. He talked liked a Cracker, but he could quote Shakespeare. Later, he would be singing an aria of opera.

Great grandfather liked Tom. But more important, Tom liked great-grandfather.

Yes, he would sell all the land south from where they stood. That turned out to be a half a mile gulf to bay from where Tween Waters is now, all the way to the curve that heads toward the Green Flash. Half a mile on what is now Captiva Drive and Millionaires Row.

Great-grandfather had a share on an island that legend has its Gasparilla had his harem and buried his ship's treasure. Captiva was now owned by a squatter and a Baptist deacon.

Now that he owned land, he needed to build a house. A house big enough to hold the eight children that they had. A dock in the bay as well as a pier in the gulf had to be built. Great grandfather got aboard the boat that day and went to Nocatee to get the lumber.

On the way back he stopped in Fort Myers and hired a contractor to build

the house. This was in May. The contractor said by January 1st of the t the year the house would be built. They would be able to move in.

Not quite.

All summer long, great-grandfather kept getting letters from the contractor. First, he had no place to live on the island. Great-grandfather told him to pitch a tent. Then the mosquitoes came. The letters got more desperate. He couldn't work in the day because the mosquitoes were so bad. He said he was going to quit, and he did.

Poor great-grandfather had to hire another contractor while up in Virginia. The next man wouldn't build the house by blueprints because he could not read them. He asked great-grandfather to tell him how many rooms he wanted and what they were going to be used for, then he would build the house. FIRED.

Finally, Tobe Bryant, who had a home on Upper Captiva (upper Captiva in those days meant the north section of the island) took over the contract.

Not only did he finish the house, but he also completed the dock. It was April 1, before the house was done. The first year, they only got to spend one month in the house before they had to head back to Bristol.

They spent all that summer getting everything ready for the next winter. All the necessities had to be bought. All the interior decorations had to be made or bought. Enough food to last the entire winter had to be bought or made.

All these items were shipped to Fort Myers. In December, my great-grandparents and four sons (plus one servant) headed to Fort Myers.

On Friday the 13th 1906, the whole mess of them sailed from Fort Myers on the mailboat. It arrived at the Captiva Bulkhead. The channel from the south end of the island was too shallow for the mailboat to get across. Tobe Bryant met them with his small motorboat.

Everything was piled on the small boat. There were five large trunks, barrels of flour, sugar and rice. There were cases of canned goods. Great-grandmother had brought smoked hams and bacon. They also had a 55-gallon drum of Karo syrup. If the boat wasn't full enough it also carried the whole family.

It was late in the day when they started out across the water. The wind was blowing very hard from the northwest. Everyone was tired and they wanted to get to shore as soon as possible. They had to get over that sandbar between the bulkhead and the island before the tide went out or the wind picked up more. As soon as they got near the sandbar they would go aground. Mr. Bryant would get overboard and pull the boat off. As soon as they would get started again, they would wind up back on the sandbar. After two hours of drifting and pulling, Mr. Bryant admitted it would be impossible to get across. He told them he would land them at the south end of the island where the water was deeper. When the wind died down, he would bring the boat to their dock.

Mr. Bryant let them off at Blind Pass. They had to walk the 3 and a half miles to the house. They carried their suitcases and the small amount of food they had bought in Fort Myers for supper. They had to fight their way through underbrush. The children were upset. They were trying to comfort the black servant who had never been out of the Shenandoah Valley.

It was well past sunset when they finally made it to the house. They found a few lamps that had been left behind the previous winter. They ate the small meal they had brought. They tucked the four boys into bed-- if you call lying on a bare mattress on the floor with a coat over you "tucked in".

The wind had gotten worse and now it was pouring rain. It would be impossible to bring the boat over in this. Great-grandfather went outside for one last look. This weather was not going to spoil his homecoming or his fishing trip the next day. He saw that one of the storm shutters had blown off. He fixed that. He and great-grandmother went to bed on their bare mattress on the floor.

They would not have been able to sleep if they knew that Friday the 13th would be a bad day.

The next morning the wind had died down and the sun came up bright. This is what they had bought the place for. Their world was primitive but that was just fine with them.

Down the trail great-grandfather could see a wagon approaching. A very sad Mr. Bryant held the reins. Great-grandfather wanted to know how a man could be sad on such a beautiful a day as this.

"You would be sad also if your boat sank during the night." Mr. Bryant said. The statement did not sink in for a minute.

"Whose boat sank?" Great grandfather asked.

"Mine." Mr. Bryant answered.

"Where?" great-grandfather inquired.

"Off the bulkhead"

"Where are my supplies?"

"On the boat"

Mr. Bryant asked great-grandfather if he would like to go down to the water and when it was low tide go and salvage what they could. He rode off in his buggy before the other man could answer.

Low tide never seemed to come. Great-grandmother worried about her down pillows, her flowered drapes, her quilts and her new Florida dresses-- all under seawater.

Great grandfather worried about his fishing tackle. He sat on the dock and waited for the tide to fall.

The high-water mark was finally reached covering the coon oysters.

Finally, the water began to recede. They realized that they hadn't eaten anything and there was nothing for them to eat because all their food was under six feet of water.

Great-grandfather stared at his island angrily. She had done about as much damage as she could do. He stood up and could see a foot of coon oysters on the piling. He started walking toward the bulkhead. He would show his island who was boss.

In the beginning he was mesmerized by the island, but not on Saturday, September 4th, 1906. He was not a happy man.

He stood on the shoreline and watched the silhouette of the boat slowly come out of the water. He could only imagine what all their belongings looked like after being underwater overnight. But his imagination didn't prepare him for the truth of the situation.

After looking at a few cases of goods, he decided to just pile it all into the cart and look at it better when they got it to the house. From the dock to the boat, they carried all the trunks, suitcases, barrels, kegs and crates to the cart. He was trying not to think how bad they were going to look in the light of day.

Great-grandmother was in her working clothes, ready to salvage what she could.

The barrel of rice was opened first, and two scoops were put in a pot to cook. The rest was spread out on paper in the sun to dry. But instead of drying, it molded and had to be thrown out. The barrel of flour and sugar did better. A crust had formed along the sides which protected the center section.

The shoes and clothes were rinsed in fresh water and put out to dry. But some of great-grandmother's best linen and dresses were completely ruined. She had packed them in colored boxes and paper. Even today there are purple, green and yellow spots on the old linens.

The only thing that had been packed in a watertight container was the cast net. When the cases of canned goods were opened, all the labels had washed off. So that whole winter, the family had "Mystery Meals".

The sinking of the boat did not dampen the spirit of adventure. They just kept rinsing and drying. But the whole affair had left a mark on great-grandmother. She was a God-fearing woman. No important decisions were ever again made on a Friday.

The home's interior was made livable as well as attractive. Great-grandmother had made so many beautiful things the summer before they came to the island. And she was aiming to make the exterior as nice as the interior.

She had to do it all herself because great-grandfather and the boys headed out each morning and did not come home until sunset. Talking with them about it was useless. All they talked about was fish and boats and boats and fish. So even the landscape was left to her.

With her first look at the barren island, she was a little wary. The beach was beautiful for sure. The rest of the island was pretty much desolate. There were some saw palmettos and an occasional sea grape. At the water's edge there were mangroves. But everything in between was pretty much empty. This was a Virginia lady who was used to hollyhock, larkspur and lawns shaded with maple trees.

The island needed an owner with a green thumb, and it had one.

First, she planted an orange grove, which did not make it. The winds blew across the island bringing with it the salt spray. With her lesson learned on planting citrus she planted things that she knew would make it. From Buck Key, great-grandmother got coconuts. She let them soak until they sprouted. These trees are now waving 50 feet above the island.

Hibiscus bushes were started from bouquets that friends brought over when they could catch a boat.

From Boca Grande (the larger island) came Captiva's greatest beauty: "The Australian Pine". She planted these seedlings all over the island. They used to grow down a five mile stretch along the beach road. Each of these huge trees started as a six-inch seedling.

I have been told by my mother Julia Elizabeth Dickey Scott that heard from her grandmother, Julia Hoffman Dickey that the pines came to the island in a different way.

My mother told me that great-grandmother told her that she got the seedlings from Thomas Edison when they had been invited to a garden party at the Edison Home on McGregor Blvd. Great-grandmother told Mr. Edison how barren the island was, and he said, "Well Julia, plant these pine seedlings and your island will be barren no more."

In one of the few Cabbage Palms on the island she found a tiny rubber tree seedling. It was eight inches high and about as big around as her finger.

She dug it out and moved it to a new location. Before the property was cleared to make way for one of the "McMansions" the tree was twelve feet in diameter and still growing.

Great-grandfather made the mistake of laying some lumber against the trunk of the tree. When they came back the next winter, the boards had been swallowed by the tree. Great grandmother had to do some fancy talking to keep her husband from chopping it down.

Captiva was a great place to raise a family. The lure of fishing, boats and the Gulf kept them busy from sunup to sundown. There were four of them. John was the oldest, then Herman, then Carl and the baby was Ernest. John was 12, Herman was 10, Carl was 7 and Ernest was 5.

Great-grandfather soon realized that keeping them all supplied with boats and fishing tackle was going to be expensive. So, he decided there would be criteria for getting a boat. Before a boy could get a boat, he had to learn to swim. It made sense that the oldest boy would get the first boat.

So, John was the first to get a boat. If the others wanted one, they would have to build it. Before the end of the first winter even little Ernest had a boat of sorts.

Sometimes an old weather-beaten boat would wash up in the mangroves. For the boys, it was like finding buried treasure. Within a week, the finder would have it scrubbed, painted and caulked. The SS John, SS Herman, SS Carl and even little Ernest would have their boat in the back bay. The boys were not allowed out in the gulf.

Every washed-up piece of driftwood ended up in somebody's boat. Their allowances were spent for caulk and paint, not on marbles and candy. Each year a new boat was added to the fleet and the boat would be handed down to the next child.

After the first winter on the island, so many of their friends came down and loved it. Therefore, great-grandfather gave away several pieces of property. Later, he sold property and the island began to develop.

In 1911, great-grandfather had so much company that he built the two-story Dickey Hotel. (This would later become the Snyder School for Boys.

Figure 1 Dickey Hotel

Herbert Binder (The Squatter) gave an acre of land for a school. After much fussing, the school board on the mainland provided some lumber.

The men on the island built the school instead of waiting for the school board to send labor over to build it.

For some reason, after a few years as a school, the building became a church. The Methodists bought the property on the advice of a visiting missionary. The creeds of the Captiva congregation are still diverse. This little church has now become the Chapel by the Sea, a church that is loved by all who visit it.

In the old days, the islanders had their church services, Christmas plays and sings. In those days each man took a turn at preaching.

Captiva now had a church and soon it would have a hotel. A painter from up north bought a lot to the north of the Dickey property. He built a little four room building with a porch.

He built it so close to the bay that when the tide came in, it flooded under the building. Since the rooms were so tiny, there was only room for a bed and a chair. The luggage had to stay out on the front porch where the threat of being washed away with the tide was a real concern.

A guest of my great-grandparents insisted on staying at the hotel. She did not want to be a bother to them, and she also wanted to be further away from the gulf. The surf made her nervous.

The next morning, she came up to the house. She was a nervous wreck. In the middle of the night, she had been awakened by horrible thumping on the floorboards underneath the bed. If she listened carefully, she could hear the water lapping under the floor. She didn't sleep much that night because she was afraid that the water would get to her and she would have to swim for her life. If she did happen to fall asleep, the thumping on the floorboards would wake her up.

When she got up in the morning and walked out on the porch, the sun was shining, the water was in the bay, and the sand was only slightly damp. The owner came out and asked her if the mullet banging on the floorboards had bothered her. He said when the tide comes in the mullet follow it. He said she would get used to it. If the sun had not been shining that day, she would have gotten on the mailboat and headed back to Virginia. But she stayed all winter.

The "hotel" blew away with the first big wind.

Because of the Friday the 13th experience and the fact that the Captivians hated to have to go all the way to the bulkhead. The people were tired of having to motor out to the bulkhead to get the mail, they hired a Mr. Harvey to dredge a channel from the Wulfurt bulkhead around the southern point of Buck Key and Captiva to the Captiva bulkhead.

After that, the mailboat and the fish boat from Punta Gorda made several runs to the island. Now sailors with a large craft did not have to worry about running aground.

Captiva's post office was a palm thatched hut. The mail was unloaded on a "dock". That word is used loosely as it was just a board across several thin pilings.

Figure 2 Reba Fitzpatrick Cottage

The mail was brought here, and this is where the core of Captiva spent their time. Everyone gathered at the post office to get their mail and learn what was going on in the rest of the world. Several tall tales would be told each day, not to be disputed by anyone.

As time went on, Captiva became "civilized". A bridge was built between Sanibel and Captiva. A real hotel was built, and people began to pour in. The social life on the island began to take off.

On Sunday everyone dressed in white. They also put on their best behavior. They would have swimming and boat races. Anything for entertainment. They had costume parties.

Fishing and boating were the ultimate past time. The world revolved around the fishing schedule. For Kingfish, breakfast was before dawn. Lunch was packed.

For Tarpon, breakfast was late, lunch was light, dinner was at five o'clock and you packed a couple of onion sandwiches for a snack in the pass at midnight.

Figure 3Dickey Family

For the tamer fish, the trip was less elaborate. The men packed their wine, food and few cooking utensils into their boats and headed for Redfish or Captiva Pass.

The women were put ashore, so they could shell or sunbathe.

Figure 4 Great grandmother to the left

The men would stroll back and forth through the pass to their heart's content. The women were quite happy because they thought these trips had been planned for them. When their husbands had caught their share of trout and blue fish, they would come back to get them.

On one of these outings, great-grandmother shocked the rest of the ladies by swimming without her stockings (a terrible show of immodesty). If she had been in the sight of the law, this would never have happened.

One late winter's afternoon, a Cuban smack anchored about a mile off the shore. His crew rowed ashore in a small skiff.

With them they brought their big dogs along with and unfortunately lice and aguardiente (whiskey). They left the dogs with my grandfather and his brothers in exchange for food and water. The lice they kept to themselves and the aguardiente they sold at a store that had been built out on the bay where all the men gathered after work.

A crew of negro men had been brought over from the mainland to put in a road from Gulf to bay. It was just at the end of the day's work that the Cubans showed up with the liquor.

The aguardiente flowed and before that night was over a man lay dead in the Captiva sand. His skull had been shattered by the blow of another who fought in self-defense.

A jury later proved that it was self-defense. The dead man's skin was white and the living man black. Many islanders were blinded by prejudice.

Great-grandfather knew nothing about what had happened until there was a knock at the study door. He opened it and peered out into the darkness. There stood a group of men with guns and lamps. He knew many of the men, but at this time they seemed like strangers. What did they want?

A man had been killed by a negro laborer. All Negros had to be off the island before night was over. If they did not, they would never work again.

They didn't know my great-grandfather very well. Over his dead body would anybody hurt a member of his household, nor would they harm any other negro worker on the island.

Great-grandfather and another man arranged to have all the negro workers on a boat headed to the mainland within an hour.

After this was accomplished, he locked his own doors-- which he had never done before. They were rusty, but he got them locked.

He took his shotgun down off the rack. In the upstairs bedroom he sat at the windowsill watching over the servant quarters down by the bay.

He heard a motorboat start up and ride away. He still did not feel secure. All night he sat with the shotgun in his lap and the shells on the windowsill.

Murder had come to the island and with it, racial prejudice. It is strange that trouble comes to even the most peaceful places in the world. White men had threatened black and great grandfather had sat at that window to protect the faithful negro servants of his household. He sat all night long waiting for something to happen. When the sun came up, nothing had happened except he had stayed awake all night.

He came downstairs to hear the servants happily singing in the kitchen, totally unaware of what had happened.

Great-grandfather paid a visit to each of the men that had come knocking at his door. Their anger had gone, and remorse had set in for what they might have done.

Captiva in those days was a magnet for drama. You had to be ingenious in everything that you did. Great grandmother had a bunch of chickens in the backyard. Each night they were being picked off by a rogue raccoon. Her chickens were the food for the winter. It was a nice break from the constant fish.

Well, my great-grandmother went and got the shotgun and killed the raccoon. Then she baked it for Sunday dinner. From then on, any raccoon stupid enough to come in her backyard took its life in its own hands.

The next native specimen on great-grandmother's hit list was the gopher tortoise. When people hear the word "gopher" they usually think of the fuzzy creature from the movie "Caddyshack". This gopher is related to the box turtle. One gopher was eating her hibiscus bushes. He became meatballs.

Little by little, the Dickeys came to realize that the abundant food on the island was better than what they were eating from the mainland. Great grandfather realized that what he was growing in his garden on the island was twice the size of the crop from his Virginia garden.

The palms were cut down to get their hearts, which made great salad. The gnarly sea grape trees became jelly. The boat loads of clams became chowder. The coon oysters became stew. The Dickey family were growing fatter.

Great grandmothers clam chowder became famous. No picnic was complete without her chowder. Many people have asked for the recipe.

A picnic in those days meant an expedition to Gault Island, which lies between Pine Island and Chino Island. It is a mass of mangroves and Calusa Indian burial mounds and when great grandfather lived on Captiva, Mr. Gault lived on this island.

Mr. Gault had been a hunter a little south of Jacksonville. He had provided venison for the larger hotels. Civilization kept pushing him further and further south. One day he found himself in the islands.

Gault's island is where all the picnics, relic hunts and expeditions took place. At least four trips a season. Captivians descended on Mr. Gault in a flotilla that was pulled by a motorboat and included at least three rowboats full of women, children and food.

Each housewife brought their best dish. (For great-grandmother of course, it was her clam chowder.)

JULIA HOFFMAN DICKEY CLAM CHOWDER

2 cans tomatoes (No. 2)
½ lb. Salt pork ground
5 large onions
2 large potatoes
4 large carrots
1 ½ dozen Florida Clams (Quahogs)

Grind the potatoes, onions and carrots. Cover with water and cook for 15 minutes after the boiling point. Add the ground salt pork after being fried. Add the tomatoes and simmer for two hours.

Add the clams that have been chopped thru a food chopper. Bring to a boil.

When trips were made to Chino or La Costa (Cayo Costa) it was suggested carefully that great-grandfather not drive the boat. It was a delicate subject and each new person on the island was told the story. The family had to discuss this, but great-grandfather was no mechanic. On his big boat, he kept a set of instructions right next to him. On the smaller 18-foot boats there were no instructions.

His sons never seemed to have any trouble starting up their motorboats, while his never started and frequently died.

Day after day he would take the little boat to Blind Pass. Day after day one of his sons would have to go and tow him back. It was humiliating for him.

One winter day he purchased a sister ship to his 18-footer. He had a little fire side chat with the four boys that it would no longer be necessary for them to come and rescue him.

"THE CUBANS ARE COMING"

Once when the Cubans landed in the spring, my great-grandfather turned the garden over to them. They pulled up carrots, radishes, turnips and one sailor spotted a cabbage and pulled it out of the ground.

The Cubans traded cigars and brandy for food and fuel.

It is told that one day, a lone man took his small boat quite a way off the Sanibel Light. His little boat only had a 2-cycle engine. Out in the middle of nowhere it broke down. The man drifted for a day and a night before being rescued by a passing Cuban smack.

On that day the marshal had decided to visit the island. Great-grandfather knew that if the marshal saw the Cubans, there would be trouble. Great-grandfather talked with the marshal and explained that the Cubans had saved the man and convinced him to let the Cubans come ashore and sell their brandy. The marshal agreed. By the time the Cubans arrived he was fishing at Red Fish pass.

Only one other arrival could outshine that of the Cubans. In April 1917, a big old barge was towed off great-grandfather's dock. Nobody seemed to know who it belonged to. Even the guide that stayed on the boat did not seem to know too much, besides that he was a Republican. Colonel Russell Cole had told him to bring the barge right there and that was what he did.

Colonel Cole was a good man, even if he was a Republican.

One Sunday, a boat came from Punta Gorda with a bunch of men wearing old denim shirts and trousers. Ropes were used as belts. They all wore shade hats that shielded their faces. But great-grandfather recognized one of the men right off. It was former President Theodore Roosevelt. Great-grandfather and family were thrilled to have him back on the island. The Democrats and the Republicans took sides on the island, but Teddy had come to fish, not talk politics. His quest was for the large Manta Ray or Devil Fish.

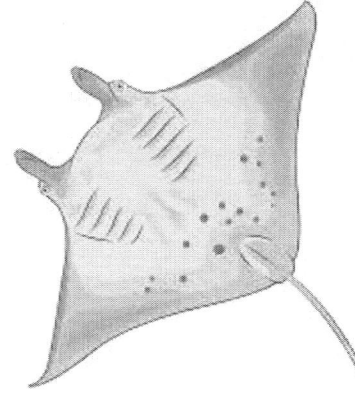

When one was sighted, the tiny guide boat would go out. It was not hard to harpoon one. The hard part was wearing it out so you could get it to shore.

Great grandfather and his sons watched from the pier in the gulf. The former president once joined the boys for a "natural" swim in the gulf.

Even today, all of Teddy's favorite fishing spots bare his name. Roosevelt Beach, Roosevelt Channel and a little spot tucked in the mangroves called Roosevelt Hole. This was the best hole for Sheepshead and Redfish in the gulf.

On April 7, the mailboat brought the news that America was at war. WWI had begun.

Roosevelt asked great-grandfather if one of the boys could take him to the mainland to see what he could do to help in the war effort.

Except for the wind and tide, Captiva never changes.

The Bubble Room by Myra Roberts

Next, I would like to tell you a few stories of the Dickey's down through the years.

Not sure what year this was. My mother Julia Elizabeth Dickey (Scott) was sent to get the mail from the Gore post office. The inside driveway was dark and scary. My Mother had heard from her sister that there was a big alligator that lived in the pond that she had to pass to get to the post office. She broke out of the underbrush, looked both ways and ran to the post office.

Another time my Aunt Mary Virginia Dickey (Barnes) had been sent to collect Sea Grapes for her mother to make jam. Halfway home she fell, and all the Sea Grapes fell in the sand. She just scooped the sand up with the berries and took them home.

My Aunt Clara Jane Dickey (Burlingham) was told if you put salt on a bird's tail you could catch it. Of course, if you are close enough to put salt on the tail, you can catch it anyway.

Uncle Carl James Dickey, Jr. was playing with my mother Julia Elizabeth Dickey Scott and his sister Mary Virginia Dickey Barnes. She ran into the boathouse and when he came out, he was staggering all over the place and was acting funny. The family didn't realize that there was a coke bottle in the boathouse that had gasoline in it. He had drunk a little bit. Aunt Mary was sent to Tween Waters to fetch the doctor. My grandmother was beside herself with worry. The doctor told her that if she didn't put a lighted match down his throat, he would be fine. My grandmother said, "I would never do that".

Another time Aunt Jane had come over to visit great grandmother on the ferry. She had a dollar bill in her hand to pay for the trip. She also was playing with a leaf. When it was time to pay, she handed the attendant the leaf and threw the dollar overboard.

CHADWICKS

In early 1923, Clarence and Rosamond Chadwick bought 400 acres at the north end of Captiva. Clarence Chadwick suffered from severe arthritis and spent many years confined to a wheelchair.

Figure 5 Mrs. Chadwick to the right

He came for the fishing. He was a banker's supply executive who invented the forgery proof paper that checks are made of.

He retired in 1925 to spend his time developing his estate. Chadwick was a Denver investor who planted the lime and coconut plantation at the north end of the island.

He frightened many people with his abrasive manner. Dottie Price Wakefield was one of the people that he frightened.

In 1935 Clarence and Rosamond were living at 427 First Street in Fort Myers.

Chadwick was born in Bloomington, Nebraska in 1877. His father, Edmond was an attorney and his wife, Isadora was a housewife.

He and his wife moved to the island in 1923 and bought up all the farms that had been destroyed in the 1921 hurricane. By 1926 Mr. Chadwick was confined to a wheelchair.

A story is told that during the Great Depression, when people were finding it tough to get by day to day, a man asked Mr. Chadwick if he could have the limes that had fallen off his trees on the ground. Mr. Chadwick said that he would rather let them rot on the ground than give them away. Not a pleasant man.

Rosamond was a trained opera singer. She tried to make up for his gruffness by being extra kind. She'd sometimes would walk the 1.3 miles or take a buggy to the Dickey House to practice her arias while great-grandmother played the piano. This piano is now on display at the Sanibel Historical Village, an 1888 Gabler.

When Mrs. Chadwick would come to practice, my mother Julia Elizabeth Dickey Scott and her brother Carl James Dickey, Jr. would try to participate from outside. They would both take their turn standing on the stump of an old Australian pine and sing at the top of their lungs. The piano was in the living room and the windows were open. Great-grandmother could hear them making all kinds of racket. One day she came out with her switch and told them to be quiet.

Another day my mother and her brother had spent an entire week building a wonderful playhouse. They had gone all over the island finding pieces of driftwood to make that wonderful little building.

Their grandmother had not really been paying attention to what they were doing. When she stepped out on the back porch and looked north, her hands flew up in the air and she screamed, "Tear it down, tear it down! It looks like an outhouse!" So, mom and Uncle Bud tore it down.

Figure 6 The Dickeys with Roosevelt

Figure 7 Carl Dickey House

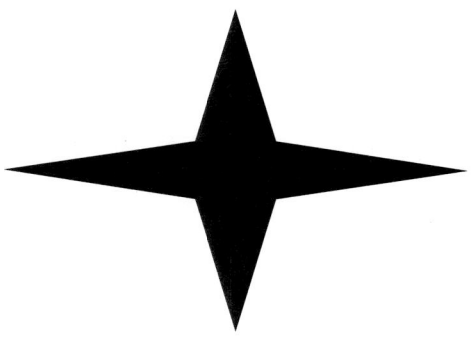

Figure 8 Carl Dickey House

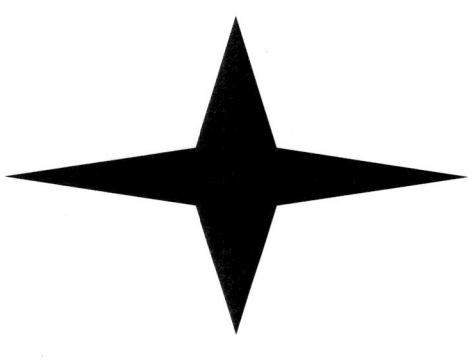

Figure 9 Dickey House

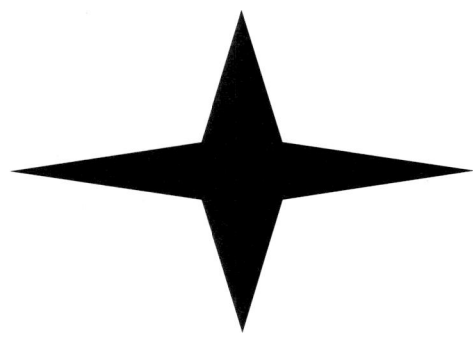

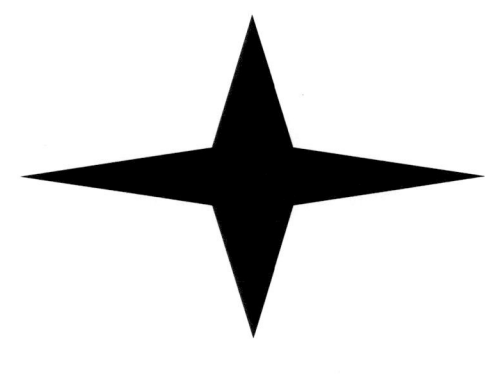

Figure 10 Dr. & Mrs. Dickey with friends

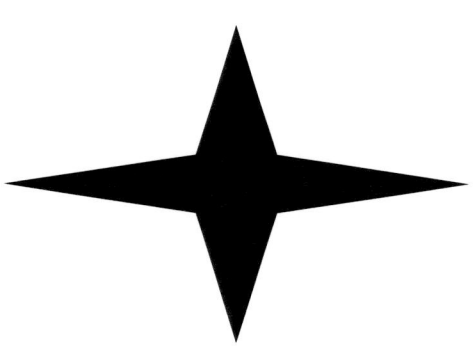

Figure 11 John R. Dickey, Jr. and his wife Maude

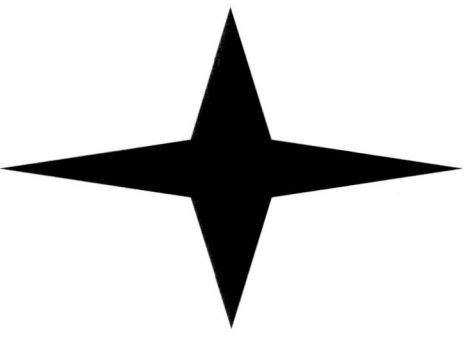

Figure 12 Party at the Dickey House

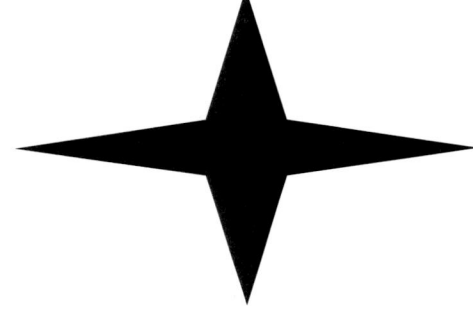

Figure 13 Dickey Pier (Captiva Historical Society)

Ding Darling by Myra Roberts

Chapter 4: JAY NORWOOD "Ding" Darling

Ding Darling (Jay Norwood Darling) was a famous political cartoonist for the Des Moines Iowa Register. He became interested in nature conservation in the 1930s. He was the founder and first president of the National Wildlife Federation and was instrumental in the development of the Cooperative Fish and Wildlife Research project. He also started the federal Duck Stamp Program. He designed the first federal duck stamp in 1934. Darling started the national wildlife refuge system during Franklin Delano Roosevelt's administration. From 1934-1935 he was the head of the U.S. Biological Survey which became the U.S. Fish and Wildlife Service. Darling obtained 20 million dollars for the wildlife project and bought 4.5 million acres for refuges. After his death, the Sanibel Wildlife Refuge was renamed in his honor.

Figure 14 Ding Darling and Belton Johnson. Captiva Historical Society

Figure 15Ding Darling, Alice O'Brien and Penny Darling

My grandfather, Carl James Dickey, Sr and Ding met on Captiva in 1935. They formed a deep friendship as well as a partnership to set aside land for nature conservancy.

This is a letter that Ding wrote to my grandfather on July 12, 1937 from Des Moines, Iowa.

Mr. Carl Dickey

Captiva, FL

Dear Carl:

I have just returned after several weeks absence and found your letter of June 10th in a big pile of unanswered mail. I am so sorry to be so late in my reply, but I presume matters move rather slowly in the summertime anyway and perhaps no harm is done.

I am glad to know that the signatures are coming in fairly well. It will be quite an accomplishment if we succeed in getting them all within the year. I note in your letter you asked what the next step and it may be that we are nearer the accomplishment of the total subscription to the petition than I think.

The original procedure as we had planned it was based somewhat on the passage of the legislative bills which Newell assured me early in the year would be successful. In that legislation, it provided that the State Conservation Commission had authority to declare refuge areas with the consent of the property owners. I am not certain that they can do this now that the legislative program failed, but we will make the attempt. At any rate, and if necessary, prepare the bill and introduce it in the next session of the legislature. If we have a special bill to declare the area included in our association a refuge, I think it would do well to make plans to include as many of the islands adjacent to Captiva and Sanibel as possible, in order that we won't have to later introduce a second bill to add to the original refuge. There is already a statute prohibiting shooting on Sanibel, but it did not declare the area a refuge nor did it specify any of the regulations which should prevail. We must be careful to include them in our next legislative measure. If I recall correctly our Constitution and By-Laws contain the kind of refuge, we contemplate, and it will not be difficult to lift that clause from our Constitution and incorporate it in the bill.

The fact that they passed the bill prohibiting netting and seining in Lee and Collier counties is all to the good. I hope we will be successful in seeing some aid to enforcement of these prohibition regulations during the coming year. That is our next step. I am certain that the State Conservation Commission will not contribute anything in the way of finance for a law enforcement warden, but if we can get them to declare our island as a state refuge, we can then materialize the promise made to me by the Bureau of Biological Survey and have it declared a national refuge. Then the Biological Survey will give us the benefit of their patronage in so far as they are able, which will be perhaps not more than once or twice a month, but it will help, and with what local assistance we can provide ought to give us pretty good protection.

I was both sorry and glad to hear that you had at last taken proper action to see that your ear was properly tended to. (My grandfather got cancer of his earlobe after working with concrete and had to have part of the ear burned off with radium treatments). Don't do anything that will slow up the healing or you will have to have it all done over again. I'd much rather have the whole island burn up than have you neglect your health.

I saw the Barkers for a minute when I was in New York, but they had very little news of the island. I wish I were down there this minute. It must be a lot more comfortable that it is up here, where the temperature has been averaging 90 to 100 for the last two weeks.

We are all well and happy and working like the devil in the hope we'll earn another vacation next winter.

Give our regards (our meaning Ding and his wife Penny) to all the folk on the island.

Yours Very Truly,

Jay N. Darling

Hawksbill Turtle by Myra Roberts

CHAPTER 5: JOSEPH B. WIGHTMAN

Joe and his family came to Captiva in 1917 from Washington state. Joe's father was George Sherman Wightman and his mother's name was Alice Ritchie. Her grandfather homesteaded on the other side of Fort Myers. They named the place after him: Fort Ritchie.

When Joe arrived on the island along with two siblings, there were approximately 40-60 people on the island, including children.

Joe said the winter homes were in what was called Dickeyville. (Named after my great-grandfather). Joe attended the Captiva School which later became the Chapel by the Sea.

His teacher was Mrs. Faidley. Besides being a teacher, she also had a Captains license.

The following children attended school with Joe: the Carters, Bryants, Mickels, the Caraways and Brian Fugot.

The schoolteacher later moved south, and Robert Knowles was the teacher.

When Joe and his family came to the islands, farming and fishing is what kept the economy going. The island was covered with citrus groves and tomato fields. The population could climb to 200 in the winter, but there were only 15 permanent farmhouses.

There were the same number of houses on Captiva in 1948 as there were in 1918.

All the grapefruit packing was done by laborers. Once they were packed in their boxes, they were hauled in a four-cylinder truck to the Alderman's store. It was north of Timmy's Nook and Bar.

In those days you could buy a side of beef for $2 and a whole pig for $5. What was even better, the seller would help you butcher it.

Joe helped around his father's farm until that age that he realized that he could do better. He decided the way to make more money was to go to California and learn to become a diesel engineer so he could work around big equipment.

So, he moved to California to get his engineers degree. He worked several places in California. In his spare time, he learned to be an electrician.

During WWII he worked as a medical and attendant with the Fifth Air Force. He was stationed in the Pacific. When he came home, he was the only electrician on the island from 1947 to 1952.

A question that many people have asked Joe over the years is how the fruit pickers followed the crops since there were no cars. Joe recounted that up until the 1920s the workers would just camp out in the fields. It could take them as much as a week to pick everything out of the grove. When they were done, they would pack up the pots and pans, bedroll and mosquito net and move to the next field. Of course, it could take a day or more to walk 20 miles to the next field.

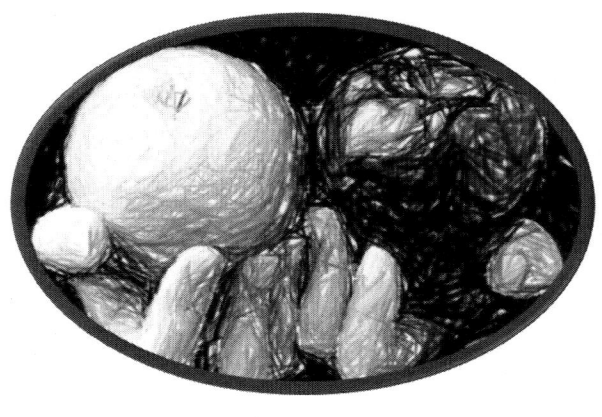

The first tractor came to the island in 1918. Before that the fields were plowed with oxen, mules and horses. It was such a big thing that the school let out early so the kids could go see the tractor.

As far as the pay scale: $1 a day for a ten-hour day. You could get $2 a day if you were a first-rate carpenter. You might make $5 or $6 a day during a good harvest season.

All the comforts of home were not lost on Captivians.

The first library on the island was in the Dickey Home. Julia Dickey and Mrs. Hicks ran the library. All island residents could check out books.

Magazines were read first by the people who bought them. They were then passed from neighbor to neighbor. Eventually they fell apart and were tossed away.

The Sears & Roebuck Catalog was a big hit. People would read it while they were waiting on the dock for the mailboat to bring it. You would sit and talk with your neighbors.

The island was pretty dependent on two main boats that serviced the islands. The Kinzie Brothers and the Punta Gorda Fish Company.

On Monday, Wednesday and Fridays the boat from the Punta Gorda Fish Company brought ice, gas and kerosene on its way to Estero. Then on Tuesday, Thursday and Saturdays the same boat would come and pick up all the fish that had been caught.

Joe said it would take three days if you had to go into Fort Myers. He said you would first get on the boat at three, you would get to town by six. All the stores would be closed so you had to spend the night. After spending the second day shopping you would head back to Captiva at night. The third day was spent giving out everything that you had brought for people.

The Dixie Line ended around 1933 and the fish company ran until the causeway was built in 1963.

Joe said the history of the island is told from hurricane to hurricane.

So, you think that is how Red Fish Pass was formed/ Not quite.

When the storm of 1921 passed, North Captiva was still connected. At high tide the little spit of land would submerge to about six inches. What finally separated it was all the motorboats dragging bottom from the Gulf to the bay separating the two.

Two years later in 1923 the gap was now much wider and so Redfish Pass was christened. At that time there were so many Redfish you could not get your hook to the bottom to catch anything else.

Hurricanes were not the only destructive weather condition. The "Northwesterners" would come in with winds and the surf in the winter. The erosion that comes from these has taken its toll on Captiva. Over the decades a sugar cane field, a mill, an artesian well, a subdivision, a long stretch of Gulf Drive and a school have fallen into the Gulf.

The first school on the island was on the Chadwick property. If it was still in the same place it would be a quarter mile out in the Gulf.

Joe tells us a little bit about Prohibition, bootleggers and rum runners.

For thirteen years from January 1920 to December 1933, America was dry due to the Volstead Act that banned alcohol.

Ninety-Nine years ago, alcohol was the drug of choice. South Florida was riddled with ports of entry for bootleggers and rum runners.

Sanibel and Captiva were right in the thick of things.

Joe said the stuff was brought in by Harry Strand who was Joe's neighbor.

Harry would take a load to Woodring Point on Sanibel. Harry had a boat that had two bait wells that were the size of a whiskey or rum crate. A trip cord was attached to the floor of each box.

The Coast Guard would look to see how far up the water line was on the boat. If they came his way, he would pull the cord and drop the crates into the Gulf.

You traded fish for Whiskey. As soon as the transaction was done, we would head for open waters.

Boats that appeared to be mullet fishermen would pull up on a site on Captiva bay side where the island was the narrowest between the body of water and Gulf on the other side. Another boat on the Gulf side faking like it was a Pompano fishing boat, would disperse its cargo to the "Mullet" boats. At night Marine patrol units would wait in the channel for nothing. As the cargo had already been delivered right under their noses.

Joe said, "One time around Christmas", Joe continued, "there were so many Coast Guard boats patrolling the channel, they could see each other." But like today with drugs, they could not do much about the Whiskey and Rum.

So now you know a little about "Shoeless" Joe Whitman, Captiva Historian.

If you would like to read more about Joe, pick up a copy of "True Tales of Old Captiva" by the Captiva Library. Or check out the Captiva Historical Society at www.captivaislandhistoricalsociety.com.

Figure 16 Chapel By The Sea Myra Roberts

CHAPTER 6: BEULAH BRAINARD WILES

I want to give you a little back story on Beulah with her family tree.

Beulah and her family lived on the island until she was 10. She attended the Captiva School where the Chapel By The Sea is now. Beulah moved to Tampa with her mother and Stepfather. He worked in the shipyards. Beulah stayed in Tampa, was married and had one daughter before she returned to the island in 1927.

There was not much to do on the island for social entertainment.

But on Sanibel there was the community house. Beulah would get back and forth to Sanibel in her 1920s Whippet.

Picture courtesy of conceptcarz.com

She traveled to the Community Center one day and met her future husband Thomas Wiles, Sr.

Beulah related that Timmy was not his name. Everyone used to call him T.M. Beulah did not like his initial name. Timmy went to an Italian barber in Fort Myers. He couldn't say T.M. well so it came out Timmy. Boy was Beulah happy that the name stuck.

In the early years of their marriage, Timmy had several jobs. He did trucking, yard work and fishing, Beulah said fishing was the worst job. It was cold, hard, rough work. But there were so many fish.

In those days the fisherman sold fish over on Pine Island. They were not sold by the pound but by the fish. So, you had to make a trip every day.

In 1940, Timmy started laying the blocks for what would become "Timmy's Nook". Beulah and Timmy ran "The Nook" up until the time of Timmy's death in 1970. Beulah's son-in-law and daughter ran it until it closed in 1994.

The Green Flash is now at this location.

Picture from Captiva Historical Society

Measuring Up By Myra Roberts

CHAPTER 4: TWEEN WATERS

I want to tell you about Tween Water's resort in the old days.

The inn started with one cottage that was originally owned by the Dickeys. This little cottage was built by the Dickey Boys, John, Herman, Carl and Ernest for their tutor Miss Reba Fitzpatrick.

Dickey

Family

Photo

The boys missed so much school when the family came to Captiva for the Winter. Miss Fitzpatrick was a teacher in Bristol, VA. They hired her to be the boys tutor so they would not be behind in their studies.

The three boys built the small cottage that served as their classroom as well as her home.

Dickey Family Photo

Bowman and Grace Price arrived on Captiva in 1924. Their daughter Dorothy was born when they went back to Bristol, VA.

Mr. Price had become quite ill, so they came south for the Winter. The first winter they stayed at Fisherman's Lodge.

They then moved to a cottage owned by Mrs. Bishop. They spent several months there, and Bowman regained his health.

In the Spring of 1925, the Prices bought the cottage that belonged to Miss Fitzpatrick. So began Tween Waters. Each year when they came down, they built a new cottage. In 1931, the little cottage became the entrance to the restaurant.

The inn started out with seven cottages. Mrs. Price ran the inn, and the restaurant and Mr. Price did the accounting and taking people out fishing.

The inn did not advertise and did not take reservations. Word of mouth is how they found their customers. Many famous people have visited the inn over the years.

Charles and Ann Lindbergh were frequent guests.

In 1936, Jay "Ding" Darling and his wife Penny discovered Tween Waters while they were traveling in their travel trailer the "Bouncing Betty". Ding was a political cartoonist as well as an advisor to presidents. Darlings' cartoons became the editorials of the day.

Until a cottage was built for them #105, the trailer was used as a studio.

In his book, "The Cruise of the Bouncing Betty", he said do not dress for dinner and the fishing is marvelous.

Darling, his wife Penny and their two children John and Mary returned each winter until the mid-fifties. Darling died in 1962 at the age of 85. His legacy of love for Captiva is preserved at Tween Waters.

Many of Ding's cartoons hang all over the resort. The sketch entitled "The Big Parade" did hang in the dining room. The drawing depicts Captiva tourists walking the beaches looking for whatever treasure they could find.

His humor would show up each year when he would sign the guestbook. Each signature was accompanied by a cartoon. One year it was a cartoon of tourists being chased by a horde of mosquitoes.

The cottage and studio that Mrs. Price rented to them still stands at Tween Waters.

Dottie Price Wakefield said that Ding and Mrs. Price were going to write a book together. Mrs. Price was the storyteller and Ding would have illustrated it. But the book was not to be.

After Bowman Price died Grace continued to run the inn. She ran the inn until 1962 when she sold it to Dottie and her husband Johnny Wakefield. The Wakefield's had divorced earlier but continued to run the inn together.

In 1969, they sold the inn to two out of state investors.

Tween Waters declined in those years. The investors had planned to destroy the inn and build 80 condos in its place.

The 1974 recession saved the inn. It was then sold to Rochester Realty Group, a Florida based firm of private investors from New York that also purchased the Captiva Beach Motel.

Purchased from the partnership of Freidberg & Hamilton out of Louisville KY in October 1976.

In 1976, Tony Lapi took over the resort and has made such a difference in preserving the history of the resort.

The first-year plans were made to enlarge the unit count by an additional 74 units, office and pool complex that was completed In 1978.

In 1980 the Sunset Room was added to the Old Captiva House.

In 1982 the Crow's Nest Lounge and Restaurant were built.

Around 1987 the Wakefield Room was built for meetings and weddings.

In 1990 employee housing was removed and 12 additional units called Mangrove were added.

Around 1995 they built the coconut building after knocking down some of the old units replacing them with 20 new one-bedroom units.

Around 2000 they replaced the older units at the sound end of the property with 4 two bedroom and 8 standard rooms now called the Areca overlooking the pool.

In 2013 a brand-new Spa & Fitness center was built.

In 2016 they took out one tennis court and built an additional pool and bar area.

In 2018 they built an entire new kitchen and did a total renovation of the Old Captiva House.

The next pages are pictures and documents graciously lent to me by Tony Lapi for the book.

The Cruise of the Bouncing Betsy

by

J.N. DARLING

A TRAILER TRAVELOGUE

Date	Our Guests	Address

Mr & Mrs Robert C Black — 437 Algonquin Pl. Webster Groves Mo

Miss Mary Grosvenor Ely — Springfield Mass

Miss Helen B. Walsh

Edward C. Ely

Penny & Jay Darling & the Bouncing Betsy. 1937

Tween Waters

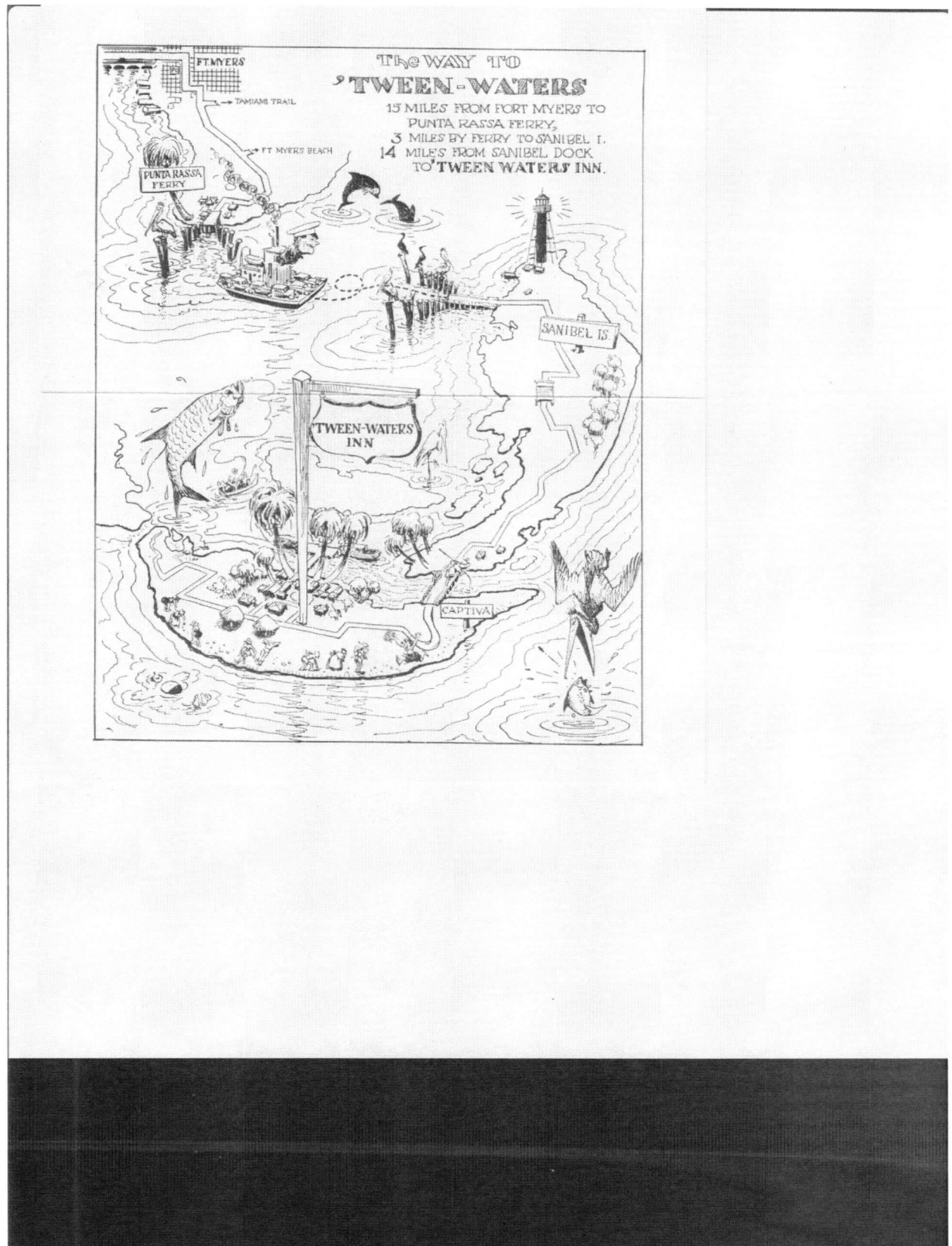

['TWEEN-WATERS] INN

CAPTIVA, FLORIDA

Here are comforts without ostentation . . . relaxation without interruption if you choose . . . the warm waters on the Gulf side of the island for bathing, and the quiet waters of the sheltered Bay side for fishing. It is quiet and informal.

Private Dock and Fishing Boats

POSTAL CARD

PLACE

STAMP

HERE

Florida WATS: 1-800-282-7560 National WATS: 1-800-223-5865

PRIVATE DOCK AND GUIDE BOATS, TWEEN WATERS INN, CAPTIVA ISLAND, FLA.

THE HEARTH BROOM SPEAKS

Come, keep the hearth with logs, and I
Shall sweep away the chaff and dirt —
As lightly as I wish the oak
Are faithful weariness and hurt!

Come, gather round the blazing fire
Forget the tedious journey past —
That peace and friendliness are here —
"Fireside Water Inn" is reached at last!

Mary Bailey
March 5 - 1935

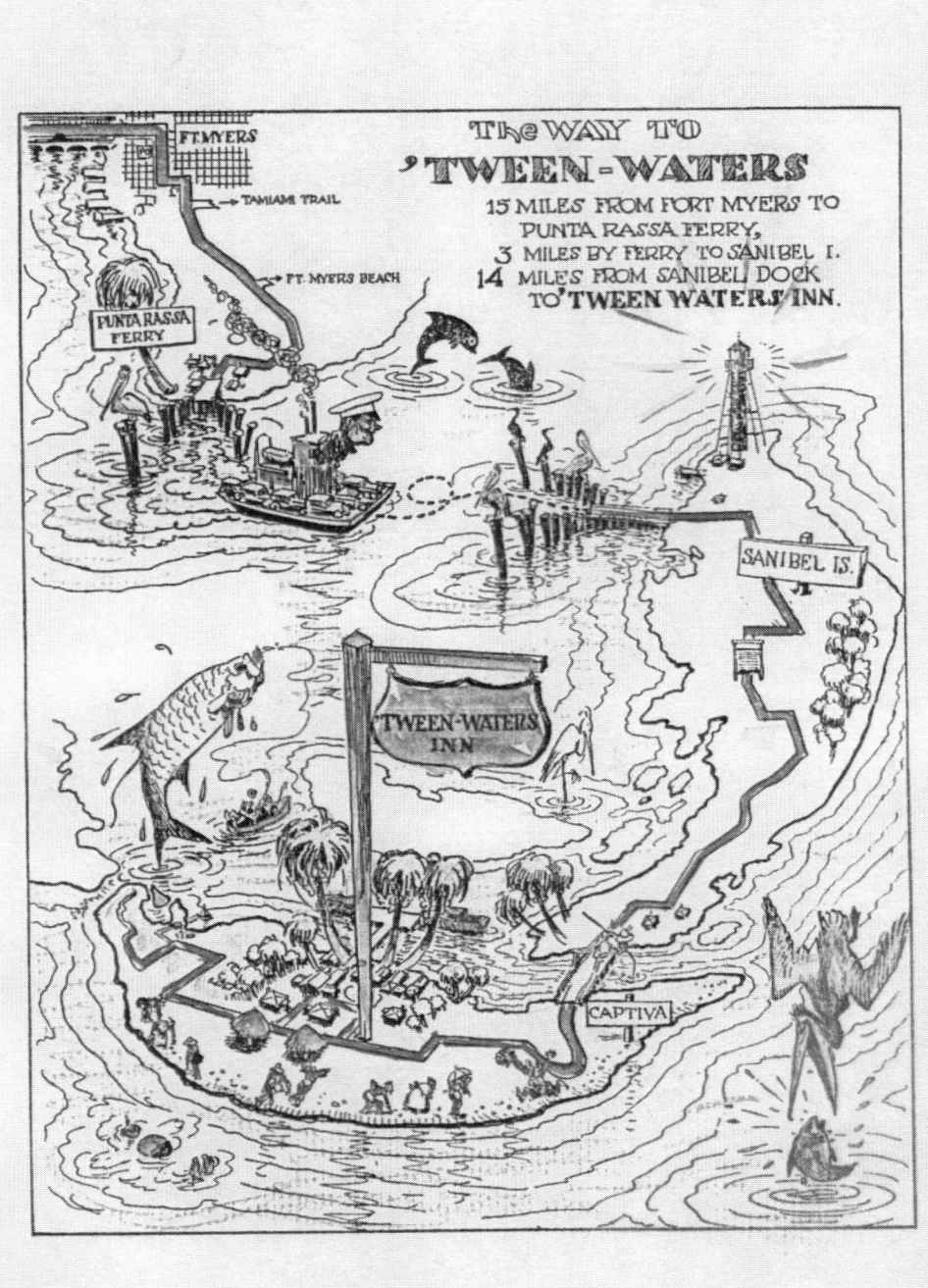

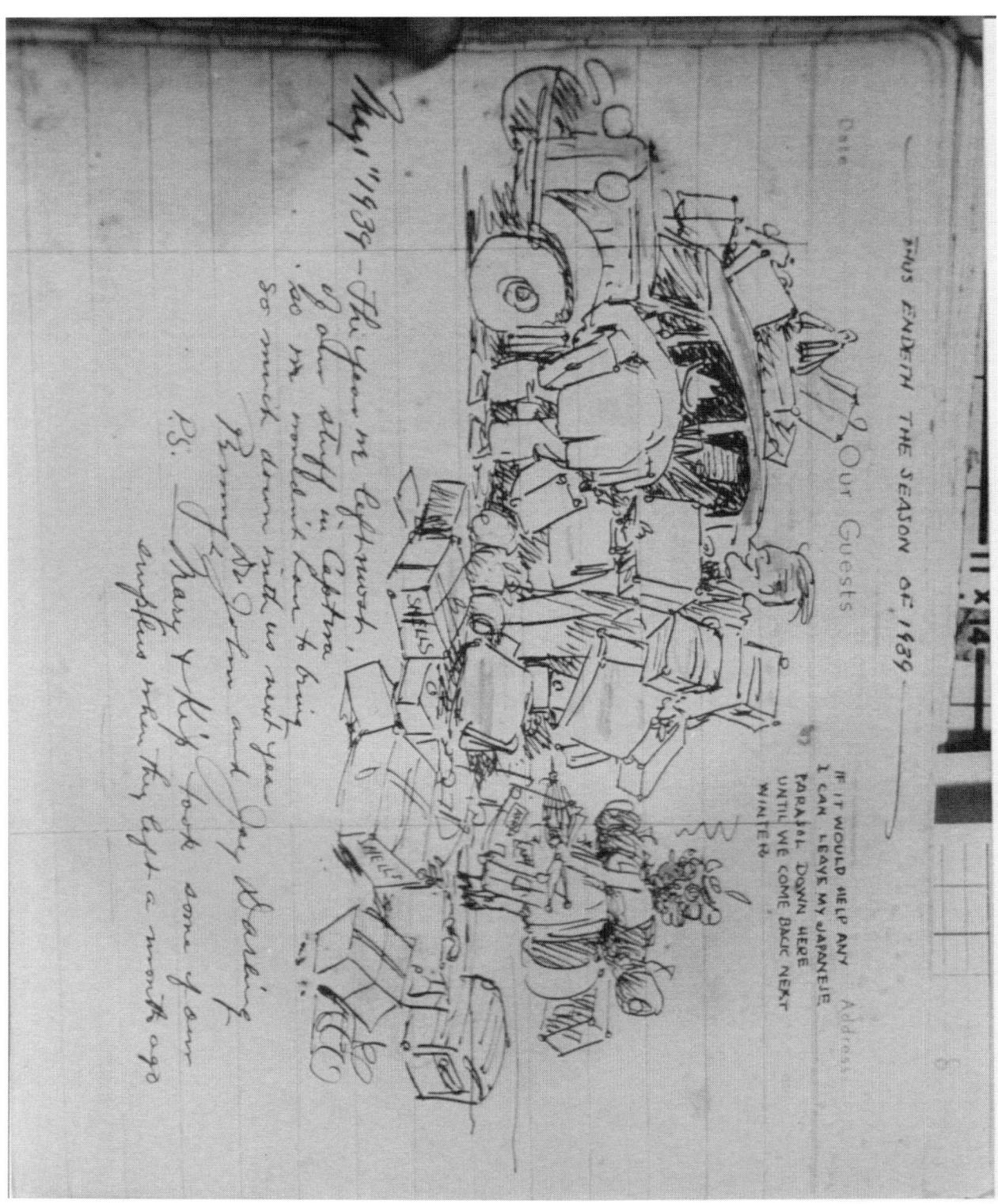

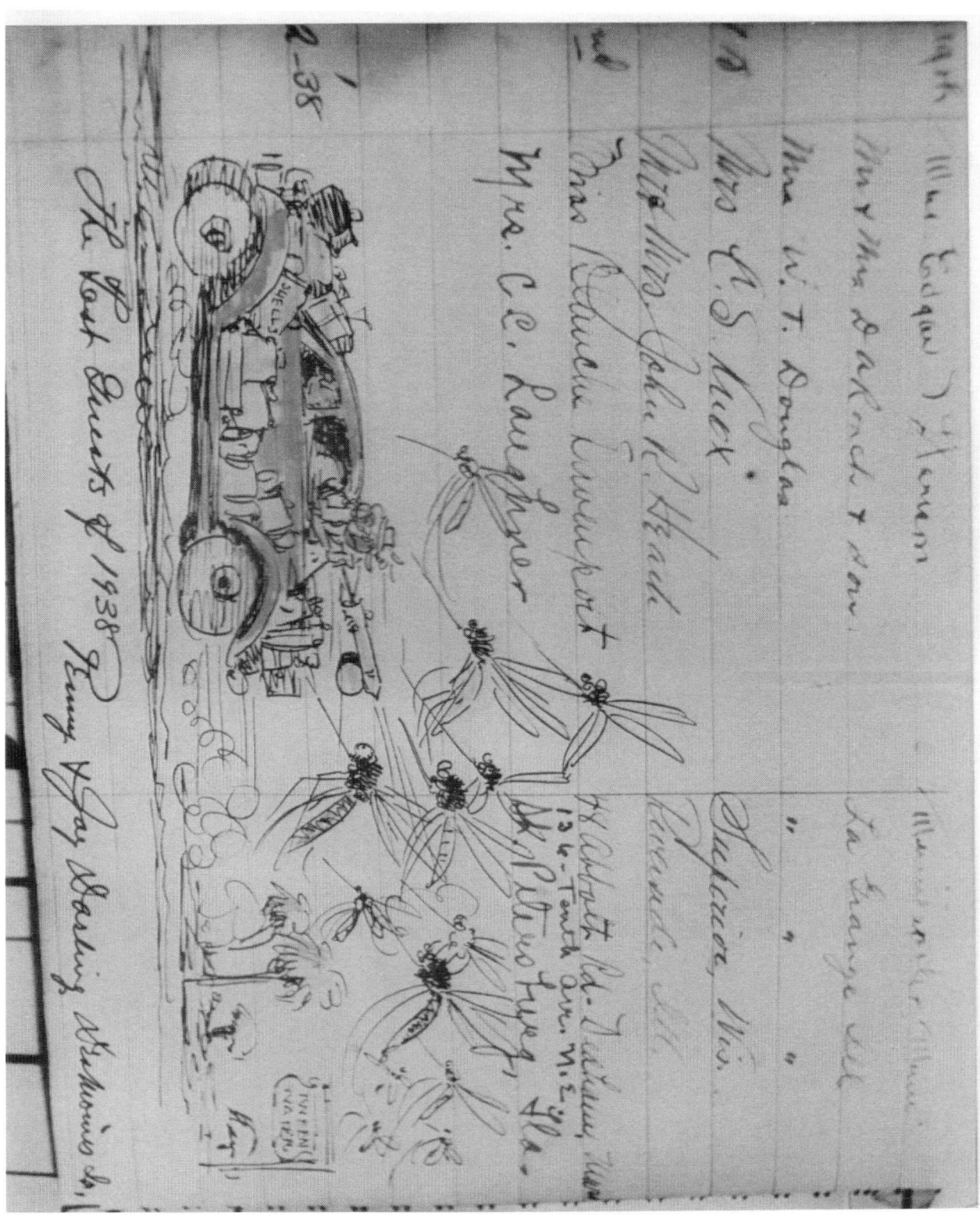

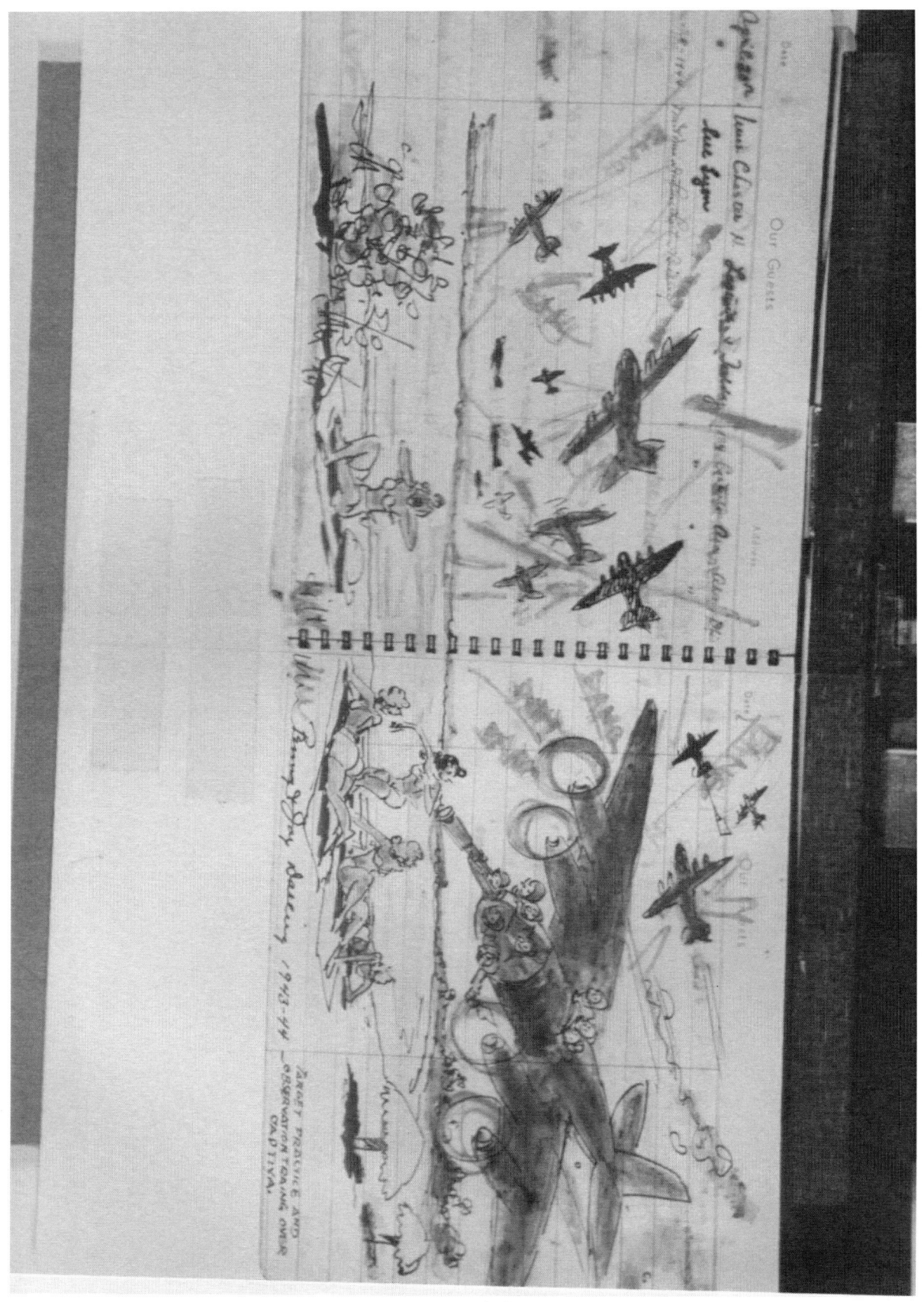

BALCH & WATSON INC.

Management Counsel
Executive Selection
612/544-0316

SHELARD PLAZA SOUTH, SUITE 352
400 SOUTH COUNTY ROAD #18
MINNEAPOLIS, MINNESOTA 55426

Tony and all

These turned out very good.
If you want any additional
copies just give a color
Xrox copy can be made from
these.

We enjoyed being with you
and hope to come back again.
Already two families from our office
are thinking about Tween Waters
for 1980.
                                    Bob Watson

They ended up costing $6.25 because
of a minimum charge.

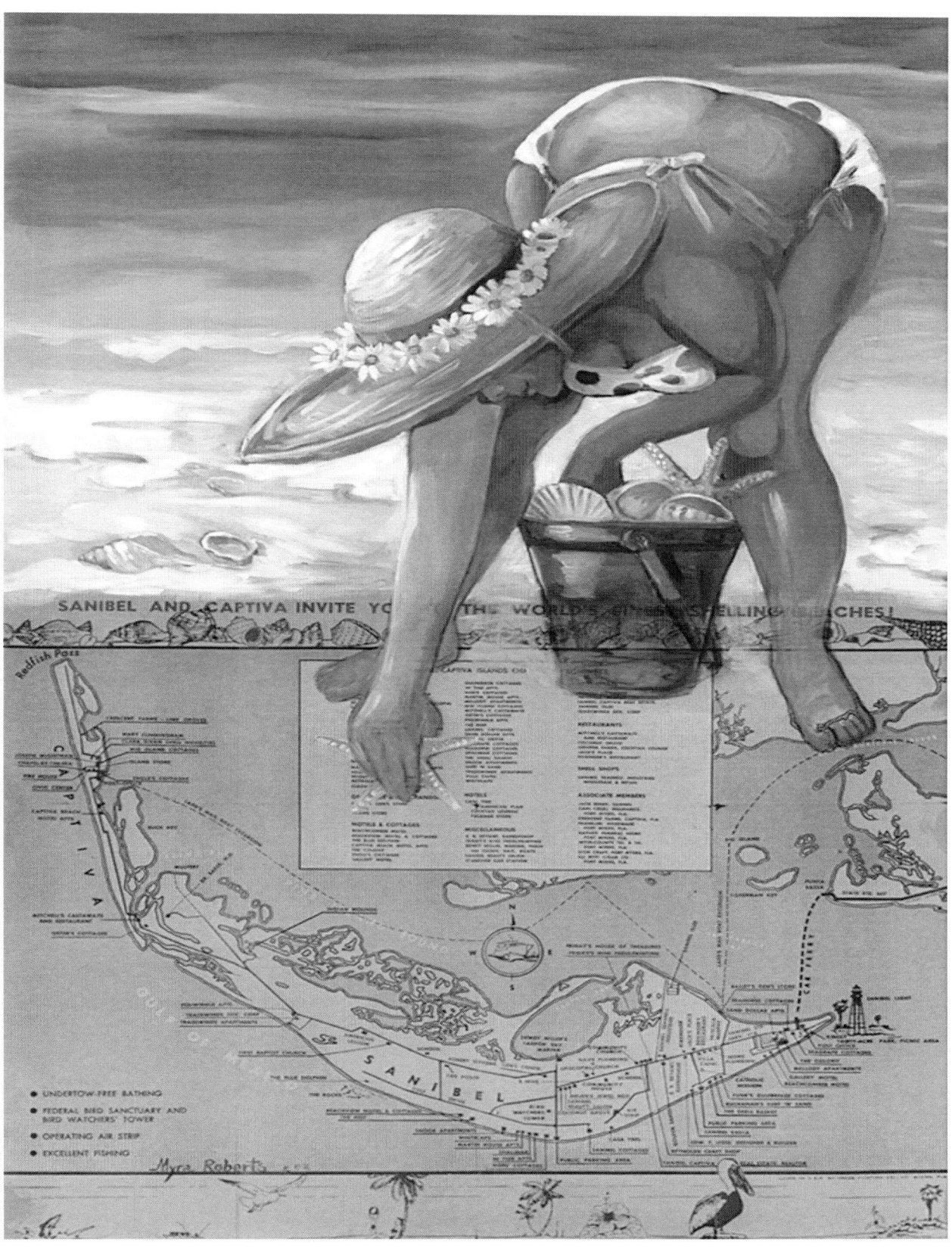

LINDBERGH COTTAGE, CAPTIVA, FLORIDA

Tween-Waters Inn -

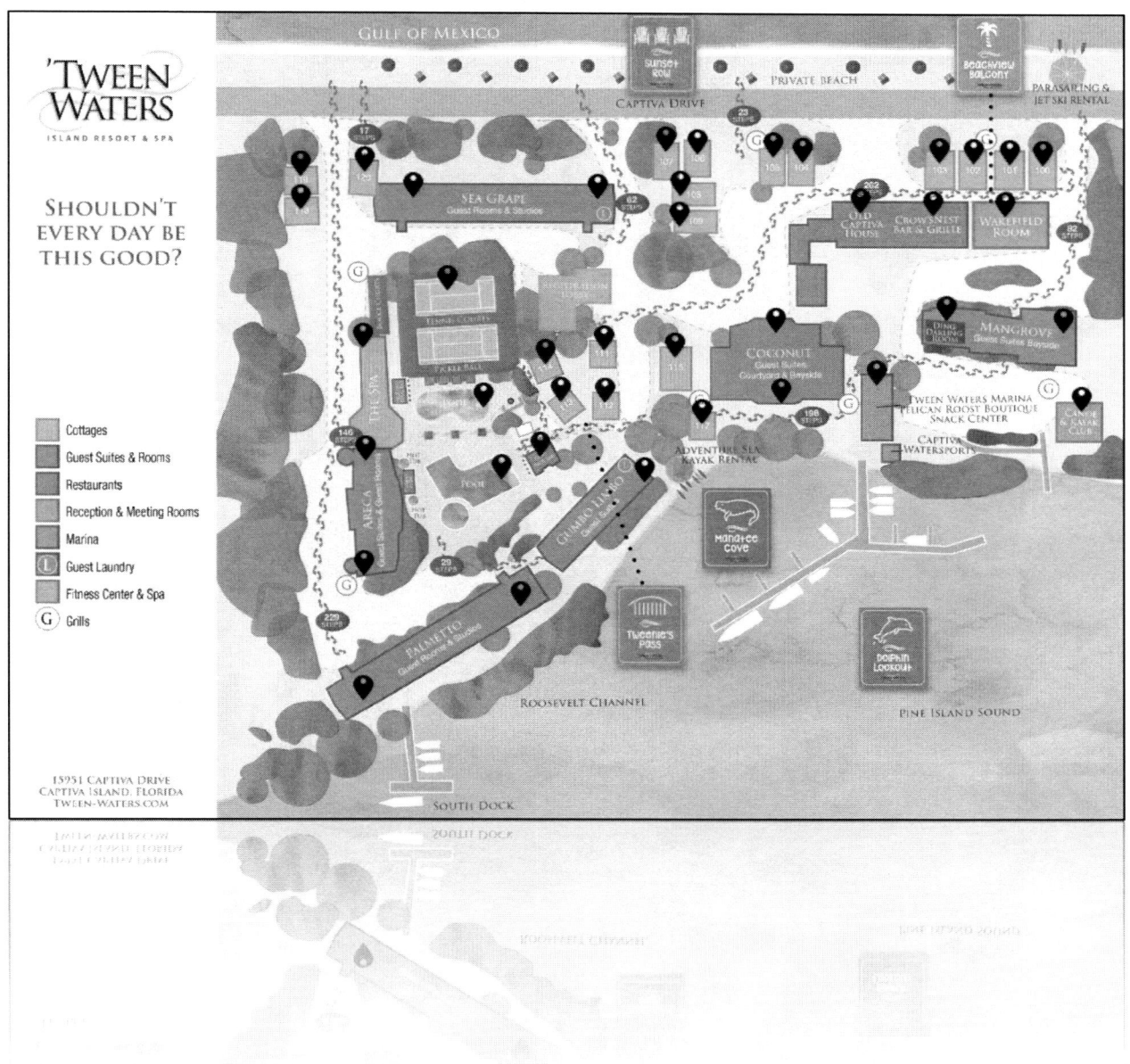

TWEEN WATERS

THIS PAGE INTENTIALLY LEFT BLANK

Esperanza Woodring by Myra Roberts

CHAPTER 8: WILLIAM HERBERT BINDER

The first person who found Captiva, found it by design. William Herbert Binder was a seaman on a ship that was hauling lumber. The boat was hit by a terrible storm and sank. Binder managed to grab on to some lumber and floated to Buck Key. He lived on Buck Key alone for many years.

We are not sure what shipwreck Binder came from.

In October of 1873 a hurricane that was later described as a "hundred-year storm". Twelve feet of water surged across Sanibel, Captiva and Punta Rassa. A small steamer called the Huntress was out in the Gulf during this storm. This was the 38-ton vessels first voyage. The boat carried building material headed for Charlotte Harbor.

It was swamped by rough seas. The boat and the cargo were lost. The cargo was worth $7000.

This could be the ship that Herbert Binder was on.

Margaret Mickle tells another tale of Binders arrival on the island.

As a young man he was on a German freighter in route to New Orleans when he was shipwrecked off Boca Grande.

He couldn't swim but managed to grab on to some boards which brought him to shore on what has been since 1921, Upper Captiva.

For several weeks, he lived on the island. He then built a raft and made his way to Pine Island. He returned home to Austria. In 1888, he returned to Captiva and homesteaded it when he was 38. For 10 years he was the only inhabitant.

I also found out in my research he was a former Army Sargent.

Binder owned the entire island of Captiva at the time the Dickeys made their first trip in 1905.

Great grandfather boated over to the island from Buck Key where the guests from the Matthews House were having a picnic. Great grandfather rowed over from Buck Key to Captiva. He walked all over the whole island. The Gulf side was beautiful, there were shells everywhere.

Great grandmother would love it. He walked to the bayside. Placid and serene.

He had to first find out how to own this paradise. It just so happened the owner of the island Herbert Binder somehow happened to find great grandfather. They walked the island together and great grandfather picked out the piece that was the highest. Mr. Binder agreed to sell him a ½ mile strip Gulf to Bay. A handshake sealed the deal. Papers would come later.

Binder and great grandfather remained friends up until the time Mr. Binder died in 1932. At the time of his death, he was living where the Jay N. Darling property was.

William H. Binder, 82 years old, resident of Captiva for 40 years, died at the Lee Memorial hospital yesterday following a brief illness. Death was caused by pneumonia which the aged man contracted while on one of his periodic visits to Fort Myers.

Funeral services will be held this afternoon with burial in the little cemetery on Captiva island in accordance with a wish expressed by Mr. Binder some time ago. N. G. Stout will officiate and Lawrence A. Powell will be in charge.

Mr. Binder, who was well known among the older residents of the country, had watched Captiva grow from an island wilderness to the present thriving little community. Settling there 40 years ago, he homesteaded practically all of the property on which the main part of the community now stands, selling it out piecemeal over a long period. For many years he had lived alone in a home near the water's edge, relinquishing all his real estate holdings except one acre upon which his home stood.

A son is the only known survivor and his whereabouts are not known. The son came here to visit his father about 15 years ago, but because of a wandering disposition he and the father had been practically estranged for some time. Friends of Mr. Binder said last night they did not know where to wire the son and tell him of his father's death. A step-daughter resides in New

(Continued on Page Five)

Faith, Hope and Charity by Myra Roberts

CHAPTER 9: MAYBELLE STAMPER

Maybelle Stamper was a very flamboyant character of the time. Even then, she led a very reclusive life. She was a world-renowned artist, but few people really knew anything about her.

She was born in 1907 in New Hampshire. Her father was a farmer. She studied art as a child. She went to Boston's School of the Museum of Fine Arts. She also attended New York's Art Student League.

In 1937 she married fellow artist William Stamper. She began teaching at the Cincinnati Art Academy. She was a rising star. Her work was being bought by the Philadelphia Museum of Art, New York's Museum of Modern Art and the Cincinnati.

The Stamper's relationship was free and easy. Each of them had casual affairs. The marriage finally ended when Bill ran off with someone. It might have been Mabelle's best friend.

Maybelle was so sensitive. She believed so faithfully in the love she had for her husband. She was also loyal to her friends. She felt betrayed. Their affair emotionally destroyed her. It drove her to become a recluse.

She was loved by both men and women. She took lovers from both sexes. But she never again gave her heart to anyone.

Other men came courting her, but she never married again. In 1955, a Mr. Van Dyne, a Dutchman employed at Scribner's Publishing proposed to her. But she flatly refused.

In her journal she wrote, "No-my fine man, you didn't quite tame me, not yet. Not quite."

In 1943, Stamper was 36 years old when she moved to Captiva. She and Bill had vacationed there.

Someone had given her a small cottage. The small lean to was next to the Chapel By The Sea. The cottage was about the size of a closet.

Maybelle prepared her meals on a portable stove. There was no plumbing.

In the Summer she would go nude. Laundry was done once a month when she would take the mailboat into Fort Myers.

This journey took all day.

This is what she wanted. There were no distractions. She could focus, meditate and create.

"I'm not interested in money." She was quoted to say. "Poverty is my choice."

If her garden did not produce what she needed. She found it in the woods. She would gather wild grass and Suriname Cherries. She loved her occasional St Paulie Girl Beer and allowed herself 10 Pall Mall cigarettes a day.

One islander that she confided in was Leslie Kowalski. They would discuss Astrology, Philosophy, Religion and time.

Mabelle was entranced by time. Kowalski recalls that she wanted to know everything about time and how it worked In her own life.

In her journal, Stamper kept up with how many minutes she meditated, gardened, ate and painted. She sent away for books on Spiritual Healing, Zen, Yoga and Philosophy. She loved Kierkegaard but also loved Agatha Christie.

Another of her good friends was conservationist and artist Sarita Van Vleck. The women spent many hours discussing Philosophy, Mysticism and plays.

Van Vleck said, "I loved talking with her." She had so many big ideas.

Van Vleck remembers one summer day she and Stamper skinny dipped.

They suddenly realized they were surrounded by sharks. They just stood quietly trying not to breathe.

The sharks eventually moved off after a school of Tarpon.

For Maybelle, every day was an adventure.

Going back a little I would like to tell you a little more about her as a person as well as an artist.

Two of my favorite articles about her were done by News-Press journalist Amy Bennett Williams and Laura Nickerson from the Cape Coral Breeze.

I will paraphrase their articles.

I will begin with Amy Bennett Williams article.

Maybelle arrived in the 1940s. At the time there were fewer than 100 people that lived on the island full time.

Maybelle was a loner as a child and the island allowed her the solitude she so desperately sought. She wanted to be alone, but her lifestyle and beauty drew unwanted attention.

When she arrived on Captiva, it was already a haven for artists and people that did not want attention. Charles and Ann Morrow Lindbergh as well as writer Edna St Vincent Millay had found the allure of the island.

While people visited, they would hear about Mabelle living there and would want to visit her. She had become one of the tourist sights. She detested being a tourist draw.

When she was walking along the road and a car came along, she would run and hide in the bushes. She would not answer her door when someone knocked.

There were few people she let into her world. And being a friend one day, did not mean you would be a friend in the future.

If you did something she didn't like, she would fire you as her friend. Sarita Van Vleck was one of those friends.

After decades of being friends Mabelle "fired" her as a friend because she was late to pick her up for an appointment.

Van Vleck had someone coming to her home to repair her air conditioner and forgot Mabelle's appointment. When she went to the house Mabelle waved her away. So ended the decades of friendship that fast.

She totally shunned contact with people in general. But the people she shunned were the people who helped her keep living on the island she loved.

Her friends would arrange cocktail parties and teas to help sell her paintings. Mabelle wanted nothing to do with the business of making money. She would watch very uncomfortably as her art was being bought.

Before Sarita had been dismissed as a friend she had helped Maybelle gather the necessary papers for her to get her Social Security. Maybelle hated anything that she had to do. Especially when it meant she had to put her shoes on.

This small check would see she and her cats did not go hungry.

By the 1980s property values on the island had skyrocketed. She could no longer pay her property taxes.

Another islander stepped in to help. Marie Dickey Kalman took overpaying her property taxes so she could stay in her home.

In 1990, when Maybelle was 82, her neighbor artist Robert Rauschenberg made a deal with her. He would buy her place and she could live the rest of her life in the house. He also agreed to pay all her living expenses.

He had his studio assistant Pam Schmidt to check in on her.

Pam and Maybelle began a friendship that enriched Pam's life.

Not that Maybelle was that easy to get along with.

Pam almost got fired once because she wanted to stay and finish painting Maybelle's house. But if she did that would interrupt Mabelle feeding her cats. Mabelle was so upset.

As her eyesight continued to fail, the whole island began to take care of her.

Parker Mills from the island store would take her food and leave it at the door. She became more and more frail.

There was no nursing homes or hospice for Mabelle. She died at home alone.

Pam found her sitting in her chair.

Pam stayed till after the EMS visit, the questions and the paperwork. Pam went home to take a shower.

"I swear, I heard Mabelle's laughter, a peal as clear as the day, a total joyful heartfelt laugh."

Now I would like to tell you a little about Mabelle as an artist.

This information comes from a wonderful article.

"For The Love of Art – Mabelle Stamper as they knew her" by Laura Nickerson.

Mabelle came from a family of artists.

Her grandfather was the famed itinerant New England stencil artist Moss Eaton. Her uncle William Richardson decorative painted almost every available surface at the 215-year-old family homestead located on a rural road between Dublin and Harrisville, NH.

Many other family members excelled at traditional handicrafts. The women were known for their quilting and weaving. The men for their woodworking.

Mabelle's love of art started early. She first studied at the New Hampshire Normal School. She then went to the School of the Museum of Fine Art in Boston. Later she attended at the Art Student League in New York.

There she studied with sculptor William Zorach, lithographer George Picher and master draftsman-painter Kinon Nicolaide.

What Stamper took from Nicolaide was the ability to work tirelessly. Never stopping for a break.

Stamper was a tall and striking young woman. In the 1920s she could be seen doing quick portraits of people on New York streets.

After 10 years in New York, she had several major exhibitions. She met, fell in love and married Wilson Stamper. They led a very sophisticated lifestyle with several good friends who summered with them in Nova Scotia.

The breakup of her marriage caused what family members called "a breakdown".

What it was she blocked out everything that was frivolous or unnecessary. Her art and her structured life were all that mattered to her. Along with her cats.

She had very few friends or relationships. Even her close friends were kept at a distance.

Even eating, shopping, feeding her cats, and gardening were structured by time. Each event was recorded in a notebook.

Everything else in her life was art.

Mabelle's closet friend to the end was Marie Dickey Kalman (my second cousin). Stamper and Marie both loved to smoke so that gave them something in common.

Marie respected Stamper's privacy.

Stamper left her entire body of work to Marie on her death.

Before removing the 800 pieces of art each was photographed and 80 were chosen for an art show.

Jensen's by Myra Roberts

CHAPTER 10: BELTON JOHNSON

Belton Johnson and his wife Miriam were close family friends. I have spent many an hour at their home on Captiva Drive. My aunt Jane Dickey Burlingham knew them even better than I. Merriam and she had been to women's retreats together.

I used to love to hear Belton tell tales of how life was like in the old days.

Jane Dickey Burlingham and Miriam Johnson at a church retreat

I found this wonderful article that Anne Mitchell from the News-Press wrote.

This article took place when Belton was 85. His memory wasn't quite what it used to be.

Belton and Merriam's house faces the Gulf. He loved sitting and watching the sun go down.

He asked Anne if she had ever seen the green flash. People say it is an optical illusion. Belton said he had seen it. It lasts for a second.

This author has seen it and it is amazing.

Belton was a charter boat captain for many years.

He gave up charters when he passed out on his boat the Lady Jane. He was hunting Blue Marlin at the time in the Bahamas. That was in 1975.

A little about Belton's background. He was born in the backwoods outside of Arcadia on Lake Blue. It was about 32 miles to the closest post office.

Belton said his father was the second homesteader in the area. They had to travel by oxen and wagon. They lived in a log cabin that his father had built.

They only went into town once a month.

Belton and his family moved to Sanibel in 1901. Belton was five.

They were farmers until the hurricane of 1921 deposited salt all over the island and ruined the farming.

His father moved away from the island and Belton took up fishing.

He made good money taking people fishing. Back then he made $12 a day and people working in the fields were making $1 a day.

He doesn't smoke or drink. His drink of choice is cola and ice.

He said storms at sea can come up real fast. He said he had been scared many times. Belton said the best you can do is talk to the Lord. "Ask him to get you safely to shore."

Belton and Miriam did not get married until 1942 when Belton was 46. Belton met Merriam when her father gave him a lift.

Merriam had a daughter Jeanette, so he became an instant father.

Merriam spent a lot of time alone as Belton was gone on fishing trips from May through October.

He and Merriam built their five-room frame house on Captiva in 1945. The home they had on the island before was destroyed in the hurricane of 1944.

Belton said a man from PA helped him frame the house. During the war years you had to wait to purchase lumber.

A fellow in Sarasota was selling a bunch of Cedar. Belton bought all that he had. When that ran out, he used Magnolia wood.

Two large tanks under the house held 13,000 gallons of rainwater that comes off the roof.

Belton has seen the beach erode. It used to be 125 feet out to the Gulf. At the writing of this article, it is only a few yards. The sea gets nearer to the door.

When hurricanes come a little bird shows up that they call "Mother Carey's Chicken". They are never around unless there is a hurricane.

J.N. "Ding" Darling was a friend and use to go fishing with Belton. Belton says he was a wonderful man but not much of a fisherman.

Belton was also Alice O'Brien's boat captain.

Belton and Miriam Johnson

Miss Charlotta's Tea Room by Myra Roberts

CHAPTER 11: ALICE O'BRIEN

Alice was an incredible person. She was born in the 1890s. Her father was a lumberman in St. Paul, MD.

She was very progressive for the time.

When she was in her early 20s, she went to Europe during WWI. Women were not allowed to fight but they could do other jobs. She volunteered her service to the American Fund for French wounded as a motor repair worker. In France she transferred to the American Red Cross.

Photo from Internet Alice is third from right.

Her first assignment was to assemble a Ford car. This was the first of her mechanical efforts.

After the battle of Chateaux Thierry, she became an auxiliary nurse to care for the wounded. She later became a truck driver. After she transferred to the truck, she transported food to the canteens.

After she returned to the states to St. Paul she traveled to China and Africa.

She found Captiva thanks to friends, the Kalmans in the 30s. She would come down and go on fishing trips. It was said she was a great fisherman. When the group would come down, they would hire boats. They stayed at the old fishing lodge. It was close to where Timmy's Nook was. It later burned.

She decided to build a house on the island. Of course, she had no problem getting wood as her father was a lumber baron.

Picture from Captiva Historical Society

About this time, she got her first yacht. She called it the Wannigan. The boat she had was named after the boat that she and her father would ride on when they would bring lumber down the river in MN.

She loved the memory of those trips with her dad.

She built her house, and it became the start of the O'Brien compound.

The Kalmans from St. Paul built a house. Mr. Kalman was a sportsman and art lover. They bought a little one-story house and fixed it up a little. Xandra Kalman lived in the house for many years.

Marie Dickey Kalman's house was a little further north near the post office.

Alice had one of the finest architects in the area design her house. It was built in the classic style out of Florida Cypress.

She built it very close to where she parked the yacht.

When her mother and aunts would come down to visit, she let them stay in the house and she stayed on the Wannigan.

The Wannigan was a large yacht. 75 feet and sea going.

Alice built a large boat slip and sea wall.

There were several houses in the O'Brien compound.

In 1941 Alice persuaded her friend J.B. Ross to come down. It was just after Pearl Harbor.

During the war years the trains were in use for the war effort. J.B. got to the island by bus then would take a sea plane piloted by Bobby Bopst.

The first trip to the island on the mailboat was exciting. You would swear you were in an exotic place. You landed at the dock that was near what was Timmy's Nook.

They would unload the mail and all the packages for the people on the island.

Most everyone on the island would come down to visit the mailboat.

Everyone would gather to hear the latest gossip from town.

Mr. & Mrs. Futch would come over from Buck Key to pick up the garbage that couldn't be buried.

They would sometimes bring over a pig they had butchered to share with everyone.

Alice would take her guests to visit Tween Waters. Mrs. Grace Price took care of all her guest and visitors. Her visitors were from all aspects of the social and non-social worlds.

Ding Darling and his wife Penny had a cabin there.

Each little cabin had a fireplace and a supply of wood.

During the war years everyone stayed in Alice's captain's house. Her captain was Norwegian, and she had built a cabin for him at the front of the property near the bay.

During WWII the Coast Guard took Alice's boat to be used in the war effort.

Living with Alice was always an adventure.

There was a primitive cook stove to cook on.

Christmas Eve was always spent with Alice.

The best part of the evening was when the carolers would come by.

Mary Bailey would play the organ and lead them.

By 1947, Alice had the Wannigan II and then later the Wannigan III.

J.B. Ross always had to go back to Vassar, so Alice would plan all kinds of trips on the yacht.

Several times they went across the state by the Caloosahatchee. They would go to Palm Beach and Fort Lauderdale.

There was always a car there to take them exploring.

One of J.B.'s favorite trips was going down the coast to the Shark River. Alice had a little boat on the deck. They would go down river and fish.

J.B.s favorite trip with Alice was when they went to the Dry Tortugas.

It had been built as a fortress. But it never ended up being used for that purpose.

It did end up becoming a federal prison. Its most famous prisoner was Dr. Mudd who took care of John Wilkes Booth, Abraham Lincoln's assassin.

Mudd was convicted to life imprisonment for this act. But he was later pardoned because he cared for the prisoners when a deadly outbreak of Cholera hit the prison. He saved many lives.

After the Norwegian captain left, Alice hired local Belton Johnson for her boat captain.

Alice also had another person on the boat. Her name was Bertha Hogstram. She did the cooking and was a companion to Alice.

Alice was the first person on the island to have a television.

Everyone would come over to watch. But the signal was terrible.

Alice had a telescope so they would watch the stars.

Alice helped so many people on the island.

She financed a little grocery store that would later become the island store.

There was also a little restaurant which Karl Wightman's mother Signe ran.

My mother Julia Elizabeth Dickey Scott said she made the most wonderful food.

Alice also helped open a small bakery on the island.

Alice shaped the lives of many people on the island.

She was a sportswoman, a fine citizen as well as a collector of fine art.

She had a huge collection of French Impression. She started collecting when they first started. She left all her artwork to the Art Museum of Minneapolis.

Alice never went to college; she went to finishing school.

She was a very religious woman. She was a Roman Catholic and very generous to the church.

Alice died in Des Moines, Iowa on her way to Captiva.

Her obituary said she had been coming to Captiva since 1932.

If you would like to learn more about Alice, check out the Captiva Historical Society online archives.

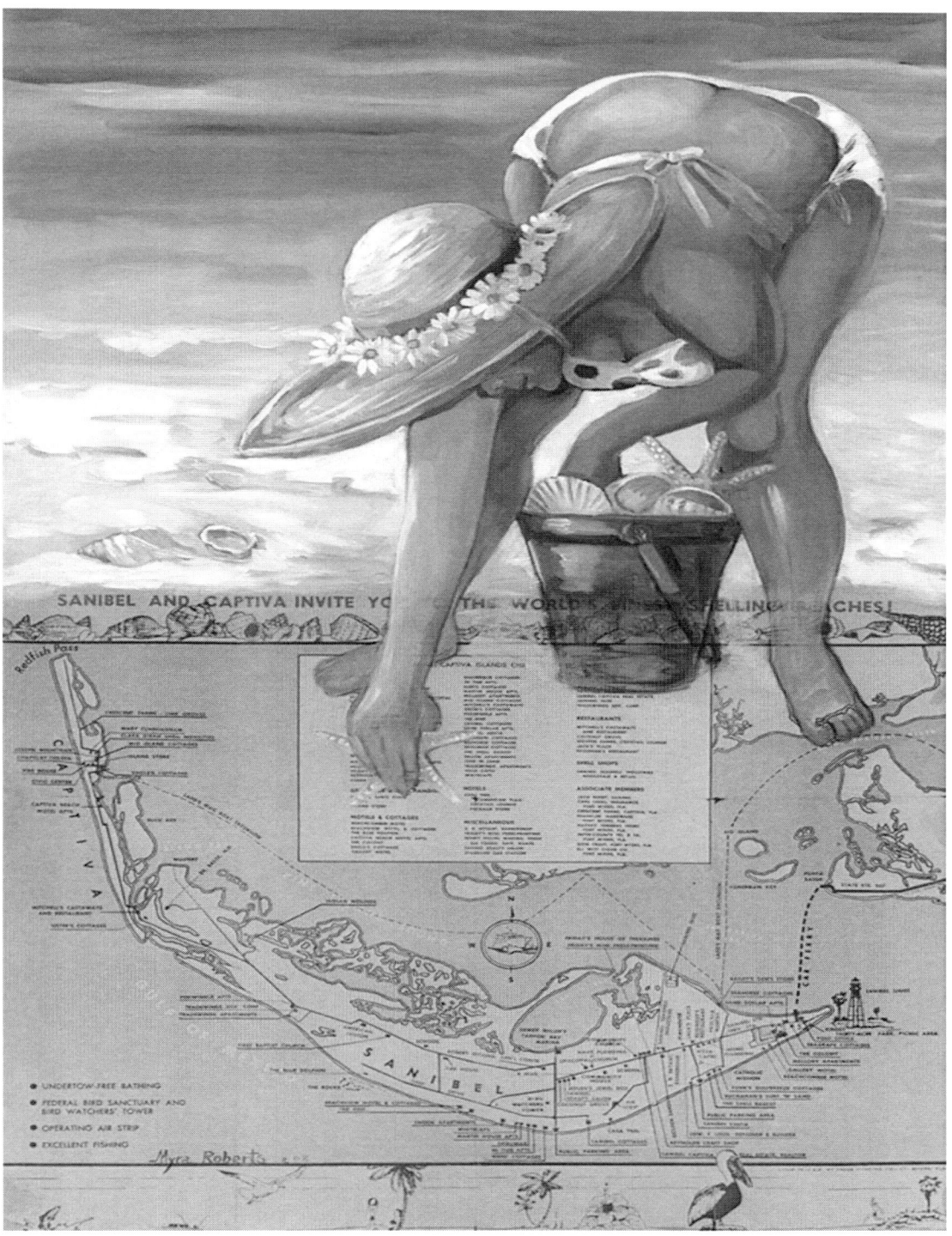

Shell Sanibel By Myra Roberts

CHAPTER 12: ANDY ROSSE

Andy Rosse and his wife Dessa were two colorful characters on the island. Andy was born in England in 1903. His family came to Tampa when he was a year old. Rosse left Tampa in 1920 when he was 16. He moved to Boca Grande and became a net fisherman. He met and married Dessa in 1924. They moved to Captiva in 1926. Andy and Dessa continued to fish. In 1935, Andy started working for Tween Waters as a fishing guide.

He loved being out on the water and taking people fishing and shelling.

Andy bought the dock in 1940. Before this the dock belonged to "Pop" Randall. "Pop" had died a couple of years earlier. Mrs. Randall wanted to sell the dock. She didn't want to sell it to anyone except Andy.

Mrs. Randall sent word to Tween Waters that she wanted to see Andy.

Andy rushed right down to see her. She wanted $800 for the dock. Andy didn't have it. He rushed back to Tween Waters to talk with Ding Darling. Andy told him the story and Darling gave him the $800.

Mrs. Randall wrote out a bill of sale. Andy owned the Captiva dock.

The island grocery store was a dock for many years. Before Andy decided with Ding Darling to move the store to what is now Andy Rosse Lane and Captiva Drive.

After the store moved, Andy turned the pier into a restaurant and bar. He had trouble finding people to work.

He turned it into a fish house. He had commercial fishermen working for him.

The Punta Gorda Fish Co. would come down three times a week to bring ice. They would pick up the fish and take them back to Punta Gorda.

The dock used to be the only place you could get a beer or rent a reliable boat.

The islanders would gather every day and wait for the mailboat to come in.

On Sunday Bobby Bopst would come in his seaplane and drop off newspapers.

It really was the social area of the island.

On Saturday nights they would have parties.

The fishermen would start bringing in their catch about noon and would just spend the rest of the day and night at the dock.

Alice O'Brien's maids told her what a fun place it was. Alice reserved the place to have a party.

Andy asked her how many people she had invited. She told him about 80.

Andy told her that the dock would fall with so many people on it. So, she adjusted her guest list. The party went off without a hitch.

Andy played the guitar, and everyone was singing and dancing.

He out drank them all that night.

Andy tells a little about how he got into the fishing business.

He came to Boca Grande on the train. Fred Wagner had a fish camp and he hired him.

He got off the train but there was nobody around. He came to the drugstore and post office and there was a man named Gus. He said a Captain Dan Futch would be going to the fish camp about 10:00.

The man dropped Andy off.

The camp was out in the middle of the water.

Andy caught Mullet, Trout, Sheepshead, Red Fish, Sting Rays and Catfish by the million.

Andy tells the hurricane of 1921 was the worst one that had hit up to that time.

Andy slept through the hurricane. The tide was six or seven feet above normal.

That is the hurricane that created Redfish Pass.

Now I would like to write a little about Dessa.

Andy was fishing out of Punta Gorda in 1924. Andy met Dessa on the old city pier. He went to visit her. Her father was a fisherman also.

She was 14 and he was 23. They wanted to get married. So, they had to take a boat into Fort Myers to the courthouse.

They first lived at Saint James. Then they moved around. Andy was still fishing until they moved to Punta Gorda. After they moved, he bought a truck and was hauling junk. He was doing pretty good at it.

He got tired of it and decided to go back to fishing. You could get 12 cents a pound and Andy would bring in 400 to 500 pounds a day.

But Dessa got tired of fishing. And when she wanted to go home, she wanted to go home Now!

In 1926, they moved to Captiva and lived way out in the bay at the fish camp.

Andy fished all day and Dessa stayed at camp which she did not like that much.

Andy and Dessa had a good life on the island.

Dessa passed first. Andy lived to be in his 80s and died in 1984.

Andy's pier is now McCarthy Marina.

If you would like to learn more about Andy and Dessa check out the archives at the Captiva Historical Society.

Relax By Myra Roberts

CHAPTER 13: ESPERANZA WOODRING

When you think of the waters around Sanibel and Captiva, your mind will turn to Esperanza Woodring.

She was a good friend. She passed in 1992 at the age of 91.

I remember many a time sitting in her living room looking out over the waters of Tarpon Bay.

One time, my mother Julia Elizabeth Dickey Scott and my aunt Jane Dickey Burlingham had come to visit her.

Her front door and back door were open as were all the windows.

We all were sitting on the couch. Aunt Jane, Esperanza and I were having coffee. My mom wasn't a coffee drinker.

I kept hearing a tapping coming from the kitchen. It sounded like something hitting metal.

I asked Esperanza what it was. She said, "it's those damn chickens, they are in the cat food again".

She had such a sense of humor. We laughed and laughed that day.

I would like to tell you a little about her history. Where she came from and what shaped her life.

She was born July 1, 1901 on Cayo Costa. She was the first born of twelve children to Manual and Rose Almas.

Her mother was a Padilla. This family homesteaded Cayo Costa.

Esperanza's grandfather came from the Canary Islands and her grandmother from Mexico. Her dad was from Spain.

Esperanza's husband Samuel Barber Woodring, Sr. was born August 6, 1880 in Potter Co., PA.

Sam was married to Aurora Dominica Aguilar and they had one son Samuel Barber Woodring, Jr.

Esperanza and Sam got married in 1917. She was 16. They moved to Woodring Point in that year.

Sam and Esperanza lived their lives on Tarpon Bay.

Both Sam and Esperanza were commercial fisherman. Sam was a bootlegger during Prohibition.

Sam died in 1942, leaving her alone to raise Preston and 5-year-old Ralph.

She became one of the islands most sought after fishing guides.

She told my Aunt Jane, my mother Julia and I a story about one of her guiding trips.

She took out a Northerner and his wife. The man kept making remarks. Esperanza told him if he didn't quit, she was going to throw him overboard. Well, he kept standing up in the boat and making remarks. She picked up her polling oar and smacked him with it and knocked him overboard.

He came up sputtering. He said, "Why did you do that?". She said, "I told you if you stood up in the boat again, I was going to knock you overboard."

Esperanza was very intelligent and loved to read.

She could throw a cast net better than any man.

She was able to keep her homestead on Woodring Point and buy additional property on Periwinkle where the Bait Box is.

Please check out photos of Esperanza done by local photographer Charles McCullough.

CHAPTER 14: BIG WINDS AND HURRICANES

There have been seven major hurricanes that have affected the islands.

Here is some very brief information about those storms.

October 17, 1910 – Accompanied by a flood tide of 10 feet on Sanibel and Captiva.

October 25, 1921 – Accompanied by a flood tide of 11 feet at Punta Rassa.

September 12, 1926 – Salt intrusion from flood put an end to farming on the islands.

October 19, 1944 – Though not as severe as that of 1921, Estero Island was submerged in 3-6 feet of water.

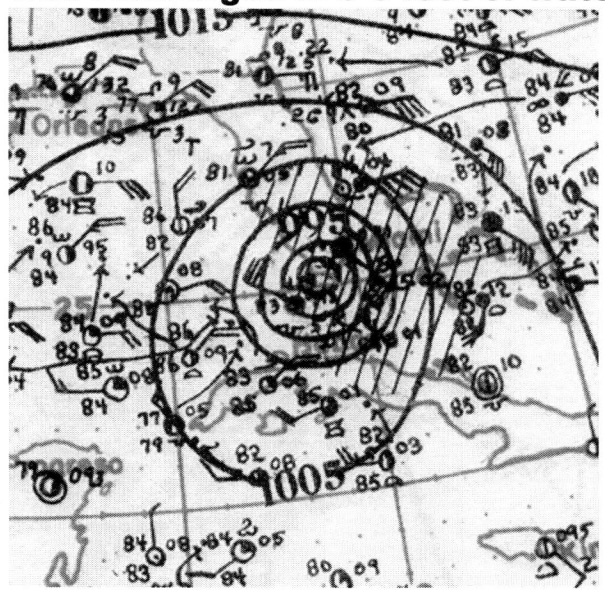

September 18, 1947 – This storm accompanied by heavy rains – 8 inches in Fort Myers; the wind reached a velocity of 120 mph on Sanibel.

September 10, 1960 - "Donna" the storm surge behind this savage hurricane brought about 16.8-foot flood tide at Everglades City; 10-11 feet at Estero. Naples endured winds gusts up to 150 mpg: Fort Myers guests of 121 mpg. Donna destroyed 319 mobile homes in Lee County. The lowest barometer reading was 27.55 at Conch Key; 28.05 in Fort Myers.

August 13, 2004 – Hurricane Charlie – This hurricane destroyed many homes on Captiva as well as Sanibel. The beautiful Australian Pines that lined the roads of both islands were destroyed.

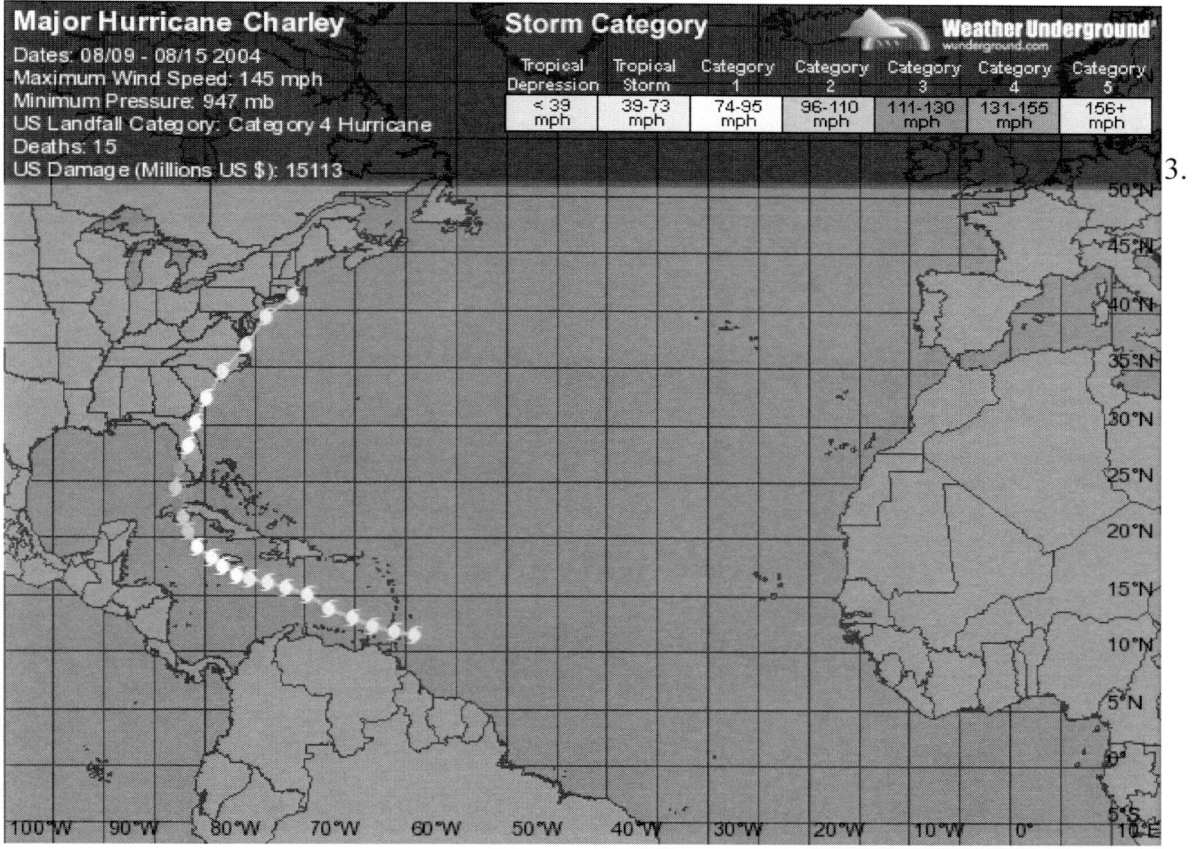

3.

Baileys by Myra Roberts

I am a 4th generation Lee countian. I have been researching and writing this book for the past two years. My mother Julia Dickey Scott wanted to write this book, but she died before she had the chance. I hope you enjoy and learn new things that you did not know about Captiva.

ISBN: 978-0-578-79162-3